Hans Wolfgang Hoffmann

The Architect's Choice

Extreme Hotels

archimap*publishers*

>>> Contents | Inhalt

>>> Introduction | Vorwort

Hotels, guesthouses, holiday homes, bungalows, guest rooms, cruise ships, caravans, campsites … these can be found everywhere, at holiday destinations all around the world. However, where should one travel to in order to mark a very special occasion or a really significant moment in life?

This volume of the series "The Architect's Choice" brings together a selection of original and individualistic accommodation establishments all over Europe, which are off the beaten tourist path and are all more than worth a visit, representing real insiders' tips. We guarantee you a very special stay, whether you are seeking to make a long overdue marriage proposal, or are simply looking for relaxation at your holiday residence.

The operators of the 40 establishments gathered in this book all display creativity and style, as well as the necessary attention to detail and genuine enthusiasm. Whether futuristic, quirky, spartan or grand, within historical walls, underground, at an airport terminal, in a trendy neighbourhood, aboard a submarine or speedboat, on rails, in a museum, or located in complete isolation—everyone will find what they are looking for, along with inspiration for an alternative holiday.

Let us know about any of your own personal discoveries! We are always gathering inspiration for the most enjoyable time of the year …

archimappublishers

Hotels, Pensionen, Hostels, Ferienhäuser, Bungalows, Fremdenzimmer, Kreuzfahrtschiffe, Wohnwagen, Zeltplätze ... gibt es wie Sand am Meer; Reiseziele auf der ganzen Welt. Wo aber hinreisen, wenn es einen ganz bestimmten Anlass oder einen wirklich wichtigen Moment im Leben gibt, den man angemessen begehen möchte?

Dieser Band der Reihe „The Architect´s Choice" stellt eine Auswahl origineller Unterkünfte in ganz Europa abseits der ausgetretenen Touristenpfade zusammen, die allesamt einen Besuch lohnen. Dabei werden echte Geheimtipps gehandelt. Wir garantieren Ihnen einen Aufenthalt der besonderen Art, führe Sie nun ein längst fälliger Hochzeitsantrag oder einfach nur der Wunsch nach Entspannung in Ihr Feriendomizil.

Die Betreiber der in diesem Buch versammelten insgesamt 40 Häuser beweisen neben Kreativität und Stil, die nötige Detailverliebtheit und echten Enthusiasmus. Ob futuristisch, schrill, spartanisch oder hochherrschaftlich, ob in historischem Gemäuer, unter Tage, direkt auf dem Flughafenterminal, im Szenekiez, an Board eines Schnell- oder U-Boots, auf Schienen, im Museum oder in aller Abgeschiedenheit gelegen, hier findet wirklich jeder, wonach er sucht.

Berichten Sie uns doch einmal von Ihren persönlichen Entdeckungen! Denn wir sammeln immer Inspirationen für die schönste Zeit des Jahres ...

archimappublishers

>>> General Map | Übersichtskarte

★ andel's Hotel Lodz

ul. Ogrodowa 17 | PL-91 065 Lodz

Tell me, Theo, have you got any idea why we wanted to go to Lodz?

Well, because of the textile industry! In any case that's what put the place on the map. In the mid-nineteenth century it attracted hordes of fortune seekers. Like that Poznanski. It seems the man didn't even have 1,000 roubles to rub together when he arrived there, but in no time at all he was a textile baron, thanks to Lodz. I must say though, Vicky, when you wanted to head there with me in 1974, nobody would have thought it would turn out the way it did! Nowadays it is more the bars and clubs that attract people. Apparently there's a greater concentration of them all around Piotrowska, the main boulevard, than anywhere else on the continent.

So has the weaving industry come to an end for good now, Theo?

Poznanski's factory complex is still in existence, now as Poland's largest Urban Entertainment Centre! It also houses the city's most expensive hotel. The architect, a certain Wojciech Poplawski, had some rather clever ideas when he designed it: he simply drilled a couple of spacey light shafts into the monument!

He left the brickwork as it was. The whole building bears the wounds of bygone days, the scars adorn all of the 277 rooms and apartments. Of course there are also all sorts of old looms lying around. And there is almost more fancy embroidery there now than in the past, custom-made by the designers Jestico + Whiles from London. It's just begging for a mega pillow fight ...

Surely it's not quite as extreme as that, Theo ...

You'll see, Vicky, next time you're there! After all, they've got the biggest party venue far and wide, in the attic. To top it all, there's the pool: a glass cube was built around the former fire extinguishing water tank and there you have it, an indoor pool. Up there the whole city is at your feet, almost like in the past ...

Alright then, Theo, we're off to Lodz! Let's go for it. And we'll throw everything we can lay our hands on! Theo ...?

Sag mal, Theo, verstehst du endlich, warum wir nach Lodz fahren wollten?

Na wegen der Textilindustrie! Jedenfalls hat die das Nest erst groß gemacht. Mitte des 19. Jahrhunderts mochte das ganze Heerscharen von Glücksrittern anziehen. So wie diesen Poznanski: Der Mann hatte angeblich keine 1.000 Rubel am Start und war doch bald – Lodz sei Dank – Weberbaron. Nur, Vicky: Wie Du 1974 mit mir los wolltest, konnte mit so was nun wirklich keiner rechnen! Mittlerweile locken ja mehr die Bars und Klubs. Rund um die Piotrkowska, den Hauptboulevard, sollen die sich ja dichter drängeln als sonst wo auf dem Kontinent.

Sag bloß, Theo, mit der Weberei ist es völlig vorbei?

Poznanskis Fabrikkomplex existiert ja noch, heute als größtes Urban Entertainment Center Polens! Auch das teuerste Hotel der Stadt hat sich da angesiedelt. Ein gewisser Wojciech Poplawski war da sehr behände: Der feine Herr Architekt hat einfach ein paar spacige Lichtschächte reingebohrt in das Denkmal! Dafür blieb der Backstein, wie er war. Das ganze Haus zeigt die Wunden von anno dazumal, die Naben zieren sämtliche 277 Zimmer und Apartments. Daneben findest du natürlich allerlei alte Webstühle. An Feinstickerei hat es hier sogar fast mehr als früher. Wurde extra herbeigeschafft, von den Designern Jestico + Whiles aus London. Das schreit nach 'ner kolossalen Kissenschlacht ...

Geh fort, Theo, so extrem geht es da gar nicht zu ...

Wart's ab, Vicky, wenn du da nochmal auftrittst! Immerhin haben die den größten Partykeller weit und breit, und zwar unter'm Dach. Getoppt wird das ganze nur durch den Pool: Ein Glaskasten um den einstigen Löschwasserspeicher – und fertig war das Hallenbad. Da oben liegt dir die ganze Stadt zu Füßen, fast so wie früher ...

Das reicht, Theo, wir fahr'n nach Lodz! Da packen wir das Glück beim Schopf! Und hauen alles auf den Kopf! Theo ...?

Booking information:

ul. Ogrodowa 17

PL-91 065 Lodz

T +48 (0)42 / 279 10 00

info@andelslodz.com

www.andelslodz.com

Natur/   Familie/   Hotel/
nature   family   hotel

★ Apafi Manor

RO-557117 Malmkrog

Do like Prince Charles of Wales and Cornwall and discover the true values you can find in Transylvania! On the way, you'll get to know Transylvania's real rulers: the Apafis. Nobel family ruled the topographically closed-off territory for centuries.

In the meantime, most of the bloodlines have been severed, but Mălâncrav is still an Apafi stronghold, with a higher concentration of Transylvanian Saxons than anywhere else.

This is also thanks to Prince Charles of Wales and Cornwall, who last called in here on 9 May 2006. He's the patron of the Mihai Eminescu Trust, that is restoring one landmark after another in Transylvania. Anglo-Saxon, German and local architects are working hand in hand to reverse the effects of decades of neglect. Consequently, some very charming guesthouses have been developed in the region that was hardly overrun by tourists in the past. The recently refurbished Apafi headquarters now has five rooms, with a highly authentic style.

Those who tire of the stately veranda have plenty of other options: on the hillsides with their orchards, at the nearby fortified church with its unusual structure, rather large for a community of 1,000 souls, or in Mălâncrav itself, whose village-like layout is similar to that of English mining towns. Many of the inhabitants exude the same irresistible charm as the Transylvanian singer Peter Maffay. In the evening, the Apafi library reveals the truth behind the vampire legend ...

<<< Facts: Prince Charles last called in here on 9 May 2006.

Machen Sie es wie Prinz Charles von Wales und Cornwall, und entdecken Sie die wahren Werte Transilvaniens! Zuvor werden Sie Siebenbürgens wahre Herrscher kennenlernen: die Apafis. Die Adelsfamilie hielt das topografisch abgeriegelte Territorium über Jahrhunderte. Mittlerweile mögen die meisten Stammbäume gekappt sein: Doch steht die der ehemalige Stammsitz der Familie nach wie vor in Malmkrog, wo es mehr Siebenbürger Sachsen gibt als irgendwo sonst. Zu danken ist das nicht zuletzt Prinz Charles von Wales und Cornwall, der zuletzt am 9. Mai 2006 vorbeischaute. Er ist des Mihai Eminescu Trust, der in Siebenbürgen ein Denkmal nach dem anderen restauriert. Hand in Hand arbeiten angelsächsische, deutsche und lokale Architekten daran, Jahrzehnte der Vernachlässigung vergessen zu machen. En passant erhält das Terrain, das in der Vergangenheit vom Tourismus nicht gerade überrannt wurde, äußerst reizvolle Unterkünfte.

So verfügt der frisch herausgeputzte Apafi-Stammsitz inzwischen über fünf Zimmer, die in Sachen Stiltreue keinen Vergleich scheuen müssen.

Wer von der hochherrschaftlichen Veranda genug hat, findet reichlich Abwechslung: in den stets Früchte tragenden Hügeln; in der unmittelbar benachbarten Kirchenburg, deren seltener Bautyp für eine 1.000-Seelen-Gemeinde ungewöhnlich groß geraten ist; in Malmkrog selbst. Nicht wenige Bewohner zeigen genau jene unwiderstehliche Herzlichkeit, die der Siebenbürger Peter Maffay in die Welt trägt. Und am Abend verrät die Apafi-Bibliothek den wahren Kern der Vampir-Legende ...

<<< Facts: Prinz Charles von Wales und Cornwall schaute hier zuletzt am 9. Mail 2006 vorbei.

Booking information:

RO-557117 Malmkrog

T +40 (0)723 / 15 08 19

guesthouses@

mihaieminescutrust.org

www.mihaieminescutrust.org

Berge/
hills

Natur/
nature

★ ArkaBarka Floating Hostel

Park Usce | RS-11070 Belgrade

It may no longer be an adventure per se to visit Belgrade, but guests choosing this base for their stay are still letting themselves in for quite an experience. Starting with the booking, which has to be made well in advance. Furthermore, getting here will test your perseverence: it is in the general direction of Park Usce, with no exact postal address and no direct access road. Cars can only get as far as 500 metres away from their destination. By public bus, you have to change several times and are then let out in the middle of the forest, but those who manage to make their way from there to the banks of the Danube can't miss it ...

However, the location more than makes up for these inconveniences: the ArkaBarka is surrounded by cosy bathing spots and fish restaurants. Above all, the Floating Hostel really is afloat! Most of the main deck is occupied by the cafeteria, which leads out onto the terrace. Both afford wonderful views over the river towards the Serbian capital, whose old town is only a twenty-minute walk away.

The guest accommodation is equally intriguing. The modernist wooden box, purpose-built five years ago and moored on the embankment, houses a mix of two to five-bed rooms. Some have private bathrooms, others don't. The accommodation conforms to the expected international standards in this price category. Its website speaks six languages for a start, so it is hardly surprising that the clientele is just as colourful a mix as the interior!

<<< Facts: "Best Hostel in Serbia!"
Antonio Can, TripAdvisor

Per se mag es kein Abenteuer mehr sein, Belgrad zu besuchen – doch wer dafür dieses Basislager wählt, wird wohl noch ein wenig davon erleben. Es beginnt mit der Reservierung, die reichlich Vorlauf verlangt. Des Weiteren bedeutet die Anreise einen Härtetest: Die grobe Richtung lautet Park Usce. Eine präzise Postadresse gibt es sowenig wie eine veritable Vorfahrt. Und der eigene Wagen hat spätestens 500 Meter vor dem Ziel ausgedient. Auch das öffentliche Bussystem lässt den Gast nach mehrfachem Umsteigen schlicht im Wald stehen. Immerhin: Wer sich von dort zum Ufer der Donau durchschlägt, kann kaum mehr fehlgehen ...

Die Location macht diese Unannehmlichkeiten mehr als wett: Das ArkaBarka befindet sich inmitten lauschiger Badestellen und Fischrestaurants. Vor allem aber: Das Floating Hostel schwimmt tatsächlich! Den Großteil des Hauptdecks nimmt die Cafeteria ein, die fließend in die Terrasse übergeht. Beide bieten einen wunderschönen Blick über den Fluss auf die serbischen Kapitale, deren Altstadt letztlich doch nur 20 Fußminuten entfernt liegt.

Genauso spannend ist das Gastwesen: die modere Holzkiste, die vor fünf Jahren eigens errichtet und am Ufer vertäut wurde, birgt einen Mix aus Zwei- bis Fünfbettzimmern. Mal mit, mal ohne private Sanitäranlagen halten sie, was international von Unterkünften dieser Preiskategorie erwartet werden darf. Und so ist – nachdem schon die Internetseite sechs Sprachen spricht – die Gästeschar genauso bunt gemischt wie das Interieur!

<<< Facts: „Best Hostel in Serbia!"
Antonio Can, TripAdvisor

Booking information:

Park Usce

Bul. Nikole Tesle b. b.

RS-11070 Belgrade

T +381 (0)64 / 925 35 07

arkabarkahostel@gmail.com

www.arkabarka.net

Hotel/ hotel   Berge/ hills   Natur/ nature

★ Arte Luise Kunsthotel

Luisenstraße 19 | D-10117 Berlin

Every other corner in Berlin is steeped in history. However, nowhere has preserved the traces of the wondrous fall of the Berlin wall more authentically than the Arte Luise! The location itself is rather revolutionary: The present-day seat of German political power is just a stone's throw away, while before reunification the Berlin Wall literally cast its shadow here.

Ist peripheral location in the past was due to the free spirits who crossed its threshold.

The "Luise Artists' House", like the whole city, truly flourished when freedom no longer ended at one's own garden fence. Everyone wanted to make their mark, but this was taken more literally at this house than anywhere else: All guests who stayed at the artists' house for any length of time decorated their room themselves, creating their own personal microcosmos.

Many of the temporary guests went on to become celebrities within the art scene, such as Gabriel Heimler, Andreas Paeslack or Elvira Bach. In the meantime, the residential work of art is not only open to its creators, but also to the wider public.

Around the turn of the millennium, the artists' house shed its skin and an art hotel emerged, with 32 unique rooms and all the other usual bells and whistles. Extensive refurbishment was required, of a rather anarchical nature, stopping only at what they couldn't get past the municipal building inspectors. The post-reunification history of Berlin wouldn't be complete without this happy end.

<<< Facts: All guests who stayed at the artists' house for any length of time decorated their room themselves.

Den Mantel der Geschichte, den mag in Berlin ja jede zweite Ecke auftragen. Doch findet sich kein Garderoben-haken, der die wundersame Wende der einstigen Mauerstadt stilechter verwahrt als das Arte Luise Kunsthotel! Schon seine Lage hat etwas Revolutionäres: Das heutige Machtzentrum Deutschlands befindet sich keinen Steinwurf entfernt, vor der Wende warf hier die Mauer buchstäblich ihre Schatten.

Der damaligen Randlage verdankt es die Immobilie, dass Freigeister sich ihrer bemächtigen konnten. Das „Künstlerheim Luise" erlebte – wie die ganze Stadt – einen regelrechten run, als die Freiheit nicht mehr am Gartenzaun endete. Allenthalben hieß es, Präsenz zu zeigen – doch nirgendwo wurde die Gebot wörtlicher genommen als hier: Jeder Gast, der auch nur etwas länger im Künstlerheim hauste, gestaltete sein Zimmer als seinen ganz persönlichen Mikrokosmos.

Viele der zwischenzeitlichen Gastarbeiter sind inzwischen Stars der Szene, etwa Gabriel Heimler, Andreas Paeslack oder Elvira Bach. Derweil ist das Gesamtkunstwerk nicht mehr nur seinen Schöpfern zugänglich, sondern jedermann. Zur Jahrtausendwende häutete sich das Künstlerheim, heraus kam ein Kunsthotel, das neben 32 unverwechselbaren Zimmern auch sonst alle Schikanen bietet.
Dafür war eine Sanierung nötig, die von manch anarchischem Abenteuer nur baupolizeilich Unbedenkliches übrig lassen mochte. Doch wäre die Geschichte des Nachwende-Berlins ohne dieses Happy End nicht komplett, geschweige denn, dass sie sich leicht erschlafen ließe

<<< Facts: Jedes Zimmer dieses besonderen Hotels wurde jeweils von einem international renommierten Künstler gestaltet.

Booking information:

Luisenstraße 19

D-10117 Berlin

T +49 (0)30 / 284 48-0

F +49 (0)30 / 284 48-448

info@luise-berlin.com

www.luise-berlin.com

Hotel/
hotel

Stadt/
city

★ Atomium – Kids Sphere

Atomiumsquare | B-1020 Brussels

Their parents have waved goodbye. Then their world becomes increasingly blurred. The LEDs twinkling on the shiny stainless steel capsule, the lights of the city and the stars all blend together in front of the Atomium's portholes. Meanwhile, inside the Kids' Sphere, Leon, Maria, Liza and Paul whoop with delight! They and their classmates will spend this night with their teacher, on a mission to find the answer to the question: What would they like the future to look like? Like this of course!

The whole atomium has been asking this question since the building was created in 1958 for the first International Exibition after the Second World War, when the cries for optimism were very loud. The engineer André Waterkeyn created an icon based on the structural form of an iron crystal, magnified 165 billion times. The elementary particle grew to a height of over 100 metres! The interiors by the architectural brothers André and Jean Polak are equally futuristic, even more so since Alicia Framis's bedrooms and Ingo Maurer's lighting design were added as part of the refurbishments in 2006. The Atomium still attracts around 600,000 visitors a year. The panoramic area and exhibition are open to the public daily. It is only the overnight accommodation that is reserved for primary school groups, which does of course make sense, as it is they who represent the future. Who else, if not they, should be given the opportunity to sleep over their spontaneous answer to the all-important question?!

<<< Facts: The panoramic area and exhibitions are open to the public daily; the overnight accommodation is reserved for primary school groups.

Die Eltern haben zum Abschied gewunken. Jetzt verschwimmt ihre Welt zusehends: Die LEDs, die aus der blitzblanken Edelstahlkapsel blinken, die Lichter der Stadt, die Sterne – vor den Bullaugen des Atomiums wird alles eins! Derweil in der Kids Sphere Leon, Marie, Liza und Paul juchzen! Sie und ihre Klassen-kameraden werden diese Nacht ganz allein sein mit sich und ihrer Mission: Welche Zukunft wollen sie? Kein Zweifel: diese hier!

Das ganze Atomium stellt diese Frage, seit das Bauwerk 1958 zur ersten Expo nach dem Zweiten Weltkrieg entstand. Der Schrei nach Optimismus war seinerzeit so unüberhörbar, dass André Waterkeyn einfach eine Eisenkristall zum Wahrzeichen aufblasen konnte: Dessen Strukturmodell vergrößerte der Ingenieur auf glatt das 165-Milliarden-Fache. Das Elementarteilchen wuchs sich auf über 100 Meter aus! Futuristisch sind auch die Interieurs der Architektenbrüder André und Jean Polak, umso mehr seit bei der Renovierung 2006 Alicia Framis' Schlafstätten sowie Ingo Maurers Lichtdesign hinzukamen. Nach wie vor saugt das Atomium jährlich gut 600.000 Besucher ein. Panoramapunkt und Ausstellungen sind tagaus, tagein für jedermann geöffnet.

Allein das Nachtlager bleibt Grundschulgruppen vorbehalten. Was ja auch sinnvoll ist: Wer sonst wäre die Zukunft? Wer, wenn nicht sie, sollte seine spontane Antwort auf die alles entscheidende Frage noch einmal überschlafen dürfen?!

<<< Facts: Der Panoramapunkt und die Ausstellungen sind durchgehend geöffnet; übernachten dürfen hier aber nur angemeldete Schulklassen.

Booking information:

Atomiumsquare

B-1020 Brussels

T +32 (0)2 / 475 47 75

F +32 (0)2 / 475 47 79

info@atomium.be

http://atomium.be

Stadt/
city

★ Attrap'Rêves

FR-Provence

This night is our night: your eyes reflect endless horizons. The whole Milky Way is orbiting around us. Millions and millions of stars are shining their light just on you. This must be paradise. We are in heaven!

Those who make this dream a reality, simply by spending a night under the stars, soon realise that even Europe's southernmost climes get uncomfortably chilly by dawn. You need a cocoon, but indoors simply isn't the same as outdoors ...

... Or is it? Pierre Stéphane Dumas concept is based on this image of paradise of sleeping under the stars. The French designer manufactures small, transparent and inflatable bubbles. For years he has been producing whole series of crystal balls the size of garages. In the meantime, the first plagiarisms have turned up from Asia.

Of the dozens of country lodgings that are customers of BubbleTree, Dumas's company, Attrap' Reves is the largest. They are located in three sites between Marseille and St. Tropez. The main site is in Allauch, while La Bouilladisse and Puget Ville are also nestled cosily into the landscape.

It is not just its spectacular coastal panorama that makes Provence an ideal location for this type of accommodation. In the plastic bubbles you live in close touch with nature, enjoying the fragrances that waft around the hills. However, the constant flow of fresh air in the bubbles prevents the atmosphere from becoming too stuffy.

Even the acoustics are not of this world. While exterior noise deflects off the bubble, the sound reverberates gently in the interior for quite a while. If you close your eyes and just listen, it really feels like you are drifting in outer space!

<<< Facts: Pierre Stéphane Dumas's concept is based on this image of paradise of sleeping under the stars.

Diese Nacht ist unsere Nacht: Deine Augen spiegeln unendliche Weiten. Um uns dreht sich die ganze Milchstraße. Millionen, Abermillionen Sterne setzen ihr Licht allein auf dich. So muss das Paradies sein. Wir sind im Himmel!

Wer diesen Traum in die Tat umsetzt, indem er einfach open-air nächtigt, stellt schnell fest: Selbst Europas südlichste Gefilde werden bis Sonnenaufgang empfindlich kühl. Ohne Kokon kommt keiner aus. Und drinnen ist nun einmal nicht draußen …

Oder doch? Auf das nackte paradiesische Panorama setzt Pierre Stéphane Dumas: Der französische Designer entwickelt transparente Traglufthallen im Miniaturformat. Seit Jahren produziert er ganze Serien von Garagen großen Kristallkugeln. Mittlerweile tauchen aus Asien erste Plagiate auf.

Von den Dutzenden Landherbergen, die Kunden von Dumas Firma BubbleTree sind, ist Attrap' Reves die größte. Zwischen Marseille und St. Tropez finden sich gleich drei Standorte. Neben dem Stammsitz Allauch sind auch La Bouilladisse und Puget Ville lieblich in die Landschaft eingebettet.

Was die Provence für diese Art Unterkunft prädestiniert, ist nicht allein ihr spektakuläres Küstenpanorama. Die Gerüche, die das Hügelland erfüllen, geben den Plastikblasen eine naturnahe Note. Ohnedies verhindert der Tragluftdurchsatz, dass die Atmosphäre allzu schnell stickig wird. Nicht von dieser Welt ist allein die Akustik. Während Außengeräusche an der Kugel abprallen, blubbert der Binnenschall lange nach. Wer die Augen schließt und nur seinen Ohrn traut, glaubt tatsächlich im All zu schweben!

<<< Facts: Der französische Designer Pierre Stéphane Dumas entwickelt transparente Traglufthallen im Miniaturformat. In diesen Plastikblasen kann man in diesen Plastikblasen übernachten.

Booking information:

FR-Provence

T +33 (0)4 / 91 72 10 89

contact@attrap-reves.com

www.attrap-reves.com

Natur/
nature

★ Clavell Tower

Kimmeridge, Dorset UK

The patient is crying for help. Nobody has yet survived the 100-metre fall from the cliff. This spectacular fall is a theme that runs through P. D. James's award-winning mystery thriller "The Black Tower". The novel, published in 1975, is based on a true story: Not only does the tower that gave the book its name actually exist, but it was threatened by such a fate itself! The real name of the patient in question is Clavell Tower.

The ornamental structure, standing by the English Channel about 250 kilometres southwest of London, had indeed seen better days. The folly built in 1830, with which John Richards Clavell adorned the country estate he had been given, had been standing empty since the First World War. The three-storey wooden structure was rotting to the core. Even the once striking façade was only a shadow of its former self.

Besides, life on the sheer coast is dangerous, especially as the Jurassic Coast is made up of layers of shale, which are slowly but surely crumbling. This might well provide interesting insights into the earliest geological periods, as befits a UNESCO World Heritage nature site, but it was hardly any consolation to the tower. It was just six metres away from certain death and the abyss was getting ever closer!

After it was denied any help from the state, its only hope lay with private initiatives. The Landmark Trust came to its rescue. It secured the tower in 2002 by rebuilding it 20 metres further inland, this time in solid stone. The accommodation it provides for two people, to recompense this capital expenditure, has proven extremely popular: last season Clavell Tower was completely booked up.

<<< Facts: "The cliff exposures along the Dorset and East Devon coast provide an almost continuous sequence of rock formations spanning the Mesozoic Era, or some 185 million years of the earth's history." UNESCO, 2011, World Heritage List

Der Patient schreit um Hilfe. Den 100-Meter-Sturz über die Klippen hat bisher noch niemand überlebt. Dieser spektakuläre Fall zieht sich durch P. D. James preisgekrönten Mistery-Krimi „The Black Tower". Die 1975 veröffentlichte Novelle beruht auf wahren Begebenheiten: Es gibt nicht nur den Titel gebenden Turm, mehr noch – besagtes Schicksal drohte ihm höchstpersönlich! Der Klarname des Pflegefalls lautet: Clavell Tower. Tatsächlich hat der Zierbau, der sich 250 Kilometer südwestlich von London über den Ärmelkanal erhebt, seinerzeit schon bessere Tage gesehen. Der Folly, mit dem John Richards Clavell 1830 das ihm geschenkte Landgut schmückte, steht seit dem Ersten Weltkrieg leer: So verrottet das dreistöckige Holzkonstrukt zum Gerippe. Auch die einst so fröhliche Fassade ist nur mehr ein Schatten ihrer selbst.

Ohnedies lebt es sich an der Steilküste gefährlich – umso mehr da die Jurassic Coast aus Schieferschichten besteht, die langsam aber kontinuierlich bröckeln. So mögen sich Einsichten in früheste Erdzeitalter ergeben, wie es sich für ein UNESCO-Weltnaturerbe geziemt. Doch was hat der Turm davon? Ihn trennen keine sechs Meter vom sicheren Tod. Und der Abgrund kommt unaufhaltsam näher!

Nachdem jede Amtshilfe zu spät kommt, bleibt nur Privatinitiative. In die Rolle des Retters schlüpft der Landmark Trust. 2002 bringt er den Turm in Sicherheit, indem er ihn grundsolide von neuem aufbaut: 20 Meter weiter landeinwärts und diesmal rein aus Stein. Die Übernachtungsmöglichkeiten für zwei Personen, die für diese kapitalen Mühen entschädigen sollen, erweisen sich als äußerst beliebt: Letzte Saison war der Clavell Tower komplett ausgebucht.

<<< Facts: Der Clavell Tower hat P. D. James 1975 zum preisgekrönten Mistery-Krimi „The Black Tower" inspiriert.

Booking information:

Kimmeridge, Dorset UK

T +44 (0)1628 - 82 59 25

info@landmarktrust.org.uk

www.landmarktrust.org.uk

Natur/ Berge/ Ferienhaus/
nature hills   holiday house

★ Crownhill Fort

Plymouth, Devon UK

Militants and pacifists unite – at Crownhill Fort! The former will be delighted with the bastion's strategic significance: to protect Devonport, Plymouth's harbour, the largest marine base in western Europe! It was from here that the Royal Navy launched its victory over the Spanish Armada in 1588. The Mayflower set sail from here in 1620 to colonise America. It was the starting point for the 1831 expedition that formed the basis of Charles Darwin's theories of evolution. Aircraft carriers and nuclear submarines set off from here in 1982 to recapture the Falkland Islands.

Pacifists, on the other hand, can look forward to a peaceful location. Since Captain Edmund DuCane completed the bastion in 1872, it has consisted predominantly of well-camouflaged ramparts. It is only the gates and crew's quarters that surface from the 16 hectares of greenery. As it is, Crownhill itself was only involved in battle once, during the German air strikes of the Second World War. The Landmark Trust repaired the damage the fort had suffered during its century of service. Up until 1992, buried tunnels were opened up and and historic canons were uncovered. However, the restoration didn't just

create a museum. The officers' wing now houses eight tourist beds, while the surrounding vaults house event venues for parties and business. The bar has live music every week.

<<< Facts: The Landmark Trust was founded in 1965 to preserve general landmarks. Funding preservation by using the buildings for accommodation was an innovative approach. Now the trust offers more than 150 guesthouses (all self-catering) in Great Britain, France and Italy. Furthermore, the concept is being emulated in Ireland, the USA and Romania.

Militarier und Kriegsgegner vereinigt euch – in Crownhill Fort! Erstere dürfen sich an der strategischen Bedeutung der Bastion ergötzen: Devonport, den Hafen von Plymouth, zu sichern, das heißt, die größte Marinebasis Westeuropas zu beschützen! Hier startete die Royal Navy 1588 ihren Siegeszug gegen die spanische Armada. Hier segelte 1620 die Mayflower los, um Amerika zu kolonisieren. Hier begann 1831 die Expedition, dank derer Charles Darwin die Evolution erklären konnte. Hier legten 1982 die Flugzeugträger und Atom-U-Boote ab, welche die Falklandinseln zurückeroberten. Kriegsgegner wiederum dürfen sich auf einen friedvollen Ort freuen. Seit Captain Edmund DuCane die Bastion 1872 fertigstellte, besteht sie mehrheitlich aus gut getarnten Wallanlagen. Lediglich Tore und Mannschaftsquartiere tauchen aus dem 16 Hektar großen Grün. Ohnehin war Crownhill selbst nur ein einziges Mal in Kampfhandlungen verstrickt: während der deutschen Luftangriffe im Zweiten Weltkrieg. Sämtliche Schäden der hundertjährigen Dienstzeit beseitigte der Landmark Trust. Bis 1992 wurden verschüttete Tunnel genauso wieder gangbar gemacht wie historische Kanonen. Doch beließ es die Restaurierung nicht beim Museum: Im Offizierstrakt entstanden acht Touristenbetten, in den Gewölben drumherum Eventlocations für Party und Gewerbe. Die Hausbar bietet wöchentlich Live-Musik.

<<< Facts: Der Landmark Trust wurde 1965 gegründet, um Denkmale der Allgemeinheit zu erhalten. Innovativ war das Ansatz, die Bewahrung durch Beherbergung zu refinanzieren. Inzwischen bietet die Stiftung weit über 150 Unterkünfte, die in Großbritannien, Frankreich und Italien liegen. Zudem hat das Modell in Irland, in den USA und Rumänien zur Nachahmung angeregt.

Booking information:

Plymouth, Devon UK

T +44 (0)1752 - 79 37 54

info@crownhillfort.co.uk

www.landmarktrust.org.uk

Natur/
nature

Berge/
hills

Ferienhaus/
holiday house

★ CUBE Savognin

Veia Sandeilas 12 | CH-7460 Savognin

As a mountain bike, I have most fun when I'm whizzing cross country, over meadows and bumpy trails, rocks and riverbeds, mud and puddles, as long as it's downhill. I'm simply not made for standing still.

Of the many places that cater for mountain bikes, the CUBE Savognin appeals to me the most. It's also called "Bikers' Heaven". The workshop team here doesn't just sit and wait for something to need repairing. No, I am taken care of every time I cross the threshold of the hotel. Freshly showered, I roll through the whole hotel on ramps, until I reach the place where I can show off my shiny splendour the most: My room is like a veritable showroom!

I have to put up with being with all the other sports equipment there, as my rider doesn't yet want to share his bedroom with me. He prefers to explore the wide range of facilities that the thoroughly modern building has to offer. Maybe he will climb up the façade of the glass cube? Maybe he's going back and forth between the sauna and the sun loungers? Or perhaps he's just chilling out. The lounge is enormous, as well as the LED screens and the fireplace, which ensure it stays pleasantly warm. As the hotel has accommodation for 270 people, it doesn't take much to fuel a party atmosphere. I expect my rider will party the night away. That's fine by me, we'll get to ride in a cable car tomorrow then!

<<< Facts: The CUBE Savognin is also called "Bikers' Heaven"—and rightly so.

Hrrrrsch! Es geht über Stock und Stein, Wiesen und Wurzeln, durch Felsen und Flussbetten, Matsch und Modder – Hauptsache hangabwärts: Das bringt mir Mountainbike, den meisten Spaß! Fürs Schattenparken bin ich nun mal nicht gemacht ...

Von den vielen Orten, die Mountainbikes mittlerweile erwarten, kommt uns das Cube-Savognin am meisten entgegen. „Bikers Heaven" ist sein zweiter Vorname. Hier wartet das Werkstattteam nicht erst darauf, dass etwas kaputt geht – nein, meine Körperpflege beginnt bereits bei jedem Betreten des Hotels. Frisch geduscht rolle ich über Rampen durch das ganze Haus. Die Reise endet schließlich, wo mein Glanz am besten zur Geltung kommt: Mein Zimmer gleicht einem veritablen Showroom!

Dort muss ich vorerst mit den übrigen Sportsachen vorlieb nehmen. Noch mag mein Fahrer nämlich das Nachtlager nicht mit mir teilen. Er erkundet lieber die mannigfaltigen Möglichkeiten, die der durch und durch moderne Bau sonst noch bietet. Vielleicht klettert er an der Fassade des Glaswürfels empor? Womöglich pendelt er zwischen Sauna und Sonnenbank? Wahrscheinlich hängt er einfach nur ab. Die Lounge ist ja riesig, ebenso die LED-Bildschirme – und die Lagerfeuer, die stets für Betriebstemperatur sorgen. Bei 270 Betten im Rücken dürfte sich der Party-Hunger auch gut selbst befeuern. Da ahne ich schon, dass mein Fahrer die Nacht durchmacht. Mir soll's recht sein, dann bringt uns morgen einfach die Bergbahn hoch hinaus!

<<< Facts: Idealer Ausgangs- bzw. Rastpunkt für ausgiebige Mountainbike-Touren.

© Eduard Hueber / ar

Booking information:

Veia Sandeilas 12

CH-7460 Savognin

T +41 (0)81 / 659 14 14

F +41 (0)81 /659 14 15

info.savognin@cube-hotels.com

reservierung.savognin@cube-hotels.com

www.cube-savognin.ch

Natur/
nature

Familie/
family

★ Eastern Comfort Hostelboat

Mühlenstraße 73–77 | D-10243 Berlin

Newcomers to the metropolis will soon feel over-whelmed: too many tourist attractions are a must see! A helping hand is required here in Berlin. Whoever clambers on board and checks in here can already tick off many of the obligatory things to do, as the hostel is located at the heart of a picture postcard setting. The TV Tower rises up ahead in its full splendour. Oberbaum Bridge lies to the rear, linking the hip districts of Kreuzberg and Friedrichshain, as well as being the stage for vegetable battles waged between the two districts. Ten steps to the left, the longest remaining section of the Berlin Wall is literally within reach. However, take one wrong step to the right and any Johnny Head-in-the-Air will end up in the Spree river, because this hostel is located on an old steamer! The location is undoubtedly a winner. So much so that the MS Eastern Comfort wasn't enough and was extended: Ist western counterpart is anchored alongside it, adding 18 further cabins to the existing 25. All the rooms are available at the attractive rates that are to be expected for a hostel, a real give-away considering their location! In the interior, the portholes are especially striking. The rest of the interior isn't worth mentioning. It is quite typical of Berlin, namely so utterly lacking in style that it passes as cool! True backpackers, who relish the even more extreme, can ignore the cabins altogether and set up their own tent on the deck. Then they only need to undo the zip to enjoy the whole Berlin panorama!

<<< Facts: "Location and experience was out of this world! When ever I come back to Berlin, this will be my new home away from home!" Customer Alliance.

Metropolen-Neulinge geraten schnell ins Schwitzen: Zu viele Sehenswürdigkeiten erscheinen als must-see! Gerade in Berlin braucht es Hilfestellung. Wer hier absteigt, erledigt einen Gutteil des Pflichtprogramms bereits beim Einchecken – das Hostel liegt inmitten der Postkartenperspektive schlechthin.

Vorn entfaltet sich der Fernsehturm in voller Pracht. Im Rücken erhebt sich die Oberbaumbrücke, welche die Szenequartiere Kreuzberg und Friedrichshain verbindet, mögen sich die beiden Milieus auf ebendiesem Bauwerk auch in Gemüseschlachten bekriegen.

Zehn Schritte nach links, und der längste Rest der Berliner Mauer ist buchstäblich zum Greifen nah. Aber ein falscher Schritt nach rechts, und Hans-Guck-in-die-Luft liegt in der Spree – denn dieses Hostel nutzt einen alten Dampfer!

Die Location ist zweifellos ein Erfolgsgarant. Kaum dass die MS Eastern Comfort nicht mehr ausreichte, wurde erweitert: Das westliche Pendant liegt direkt nebenan und ergänzt die 25 vorhandenen Kabinen um 18 weitere. Alle Zimmer sind so preiswert, wie man das von einem Hostel erwarten darf – für diese Lage geradezu geschenkt!

Innen bestechen vor allem die Bullaugenfenster. Über das übrige Interieur ließe sich leicht schweigen. Tatsächlich ist es höchst typisch für Berlin – nämlich so dermaßen stillos, das es schon wieder als cool durchgeht! Veritable Backpacker, die es noch extremer lieben, lassen die Kajüten links liegen. Stattdessen schlagen sie an Deck ihr eigenes Zelt auf. Für das ganze Panorama Berlins genügt dann ein Ruck am Reißverschluss!

<<< Facts: „Location and experience was out of this world! When ever I come back to Berlin, this will be my new home away from home!" Einer von 268 positiven Erfahrungsberichten der Customer Alliance.

Booking information:

Mühlenstraße 73–77

D-10243 Berlin

T +49 (0)30 66 76 38 06

F +49 (0)30 66 76 38 05

captn@eastern-comfort.com

www.eastern-comfort.com

Stadt/
city

Natur/
nature

★ Ecopod Boutique Retreat

Lettershuna Appin | UK-PA38 4BL Argyll, Scotland

Who would have thought that such a dramatic duel could take place right here, of all places?! Loch Linnhe is such a peaceful spot on the west coast of Scotland, characterised by gently rolling waves and tame hills. Countless islands and fjords shield the inland sea from the vast North Atlantic.

But then there's Castle Stalker, with its four weather-beaten, stony storeys reaching up into the sky. It is propped up by one of the smallest islets, which isn't even an islet at low tide and hasn't got a name. Movie buffs are familiar with this mixture of residential castle and fortified tower: It was the setting for the bloodthirsty finale of Monty Python and the Holy Grail, as well as for Highlander: Endgame. In real life, Castle Stalker is still hanging on, looking grimly towards the opposite shore in anticipation of the first shot.

Vis-à-vis the bullets are already at the ready, cleverly concealed between birch trees and rhododendrons. It is only upon closer inspection that one can appreciate their size. What looks like an alien invasion is called Ecopod Boutique Retreat and is indeed waging a war —for sustainable tourism!

The two (soon to be three) Ecopods brandish a state-of-the-art arsenal of weapons for saving energy. The furniture consists mostly of used modern classics.

All waste is disposed of biodynamically on site. A wind turbine and solar panels are planned to supply hot water and electricity, while compressed wood is already used to increase the heating value of the fireplaces. Their ecological impact is reduced further by their basic structure, which the Berlin company Zendome based on Buckminster Fuller's ideas. Their spherical shape provides two people with a maximum of space within a minimal surface area. The insulating double outer shell limits heat loss. To preserve the landscape, the structures are supported on wooden stilts and platforms. They can also be completely dismantled. Thus the knights of sustainability will avoid a big showdown. Castle Stalker can wait for it for another 700 years ...

<<< Facts: "If David Attenborough were to ever narrate a James Bond movie, Ecopod is the perfect setting!" The Glass Magazine, 2011

Wer hätte gedacht, dass ausgerechnet hier so ein dramatisches Duell ansteht?! Loch Linnhe ist so ein friedlicher Fleck an der Westküste Schottlands: Sanfte Wellen wechseln mit wenig wilden Hügeln. Zahllose Inseln und Fjorde schirmen das Binnenmeer gegen den Nordatlantik ab und verleugnen seine gigantischen Ausmaße.

Doch dann ist da Castle Stalker: Auf mit dem kleinsten Eiland, das bei Ebbe gar keins ist und ohne Namen auskommt, stemmt es vier verwitterte Stockwerke Stein gen Himmel. Die Mischung aus Wohnburg und Wehrturm ist Cineasten wohlbekannt: Hier fand „Monty Python and the Holy Grail" sein blutrünstiges Finale, ebenso das H„Highlander – Endgame". Im wahren Leben lauert Castle Stalker noch: In Erwartung des ersten Schusses schaut es grimmig zum anderen Ufer.

Vis-à-vis liegen schon Kugeln bereit. Geschickt tarnen sie sich zwischen Birken und Rhododendren. Erst der zweite Blick offenbart ihre Übermannsgröße. Was sich wie eine Alien-Invasion ausnimmt, nennt sich Ecopod Boutique Retreat und streitet tatsächlich – für nachhaltigen Tourismus! Zur Energieeinsparung breiten die zwei (bald drei) Ecopods das brandaktuelle Arsenal aus: Das Mobiliar dominieren gebrauchte Klassiker der Moderne. Alle Abfälle werden noch auf dem Grundstück biodynamisch entsorgt. Für Warmwasser- und Stromzufuhr sind Windrad und Sonnenkollektoren in Planung, schon jetzt steigert Pressholz den Brennwert der Kamine.

Den ökologischen Fußabdruck mindert auch die Grundkonstruktion, welche die Berliner Firma Zendome aus Ideen Buckminster Fullers ableitete. Ihre Kugelform bietet zwei Personen maximalen Lebensraum bei minimaler Oberfläche; die Doppelhaut dämmt Wärmeverluste. Die Versiegelung der Landschaft verringert, dass sich die Gebilde auf Holzpfählen und Terrassen abstützen sowie komplett demontierbar sind. So werden die Ritter der Nachhaltigkeit dem Showdown letztlich aus dem Weg gehen. Castle Stalker mag weitere 700 Jahre darauf warten ...

<<< Facts: „If David Attenborough were to ever narrate a James Bond movie, Ecopod is the perfect setting!" The Glass Magazine, 2011

Booking information:

Lettershuna Appin

UK-PA38 4BL Argyll, Scotland

T +44 (0)1631 / 73 05 39

T +44 (0)7725 / 40 90 03

info@domesweetdome.co.uk

www.domesweetdome.co.uk

Berge/
hills

Natur/
nature

★ Gothic Temple

Stowe, Buckinghamshire UK

"Have we met before?" This question is not a cliché in this case. The Gothic Temple and its surroundings have appeared in a number of films, including blockbusters such as "Indiana Jones – The Last Crusade", or "James Bond – The World Is Not Enough". This is due to its location: the film set lies halfway between London and Birmingham, on the doorstep of the majority of British film studios. In addition, the location's picturesque qualities are second to none.

The Gothic Temple was built in 1748 by James Gibbs. He laid the cope stone of Stowe House, which was planned a century before as a gigantic castle. However, the surrounding 200 hectares display a far greater masterpiece, developed by Charles Bridgeman, William Kent and Lancelot Capability Brown from 1718. The three landscaping pioneers laid ponds and pathways. There are also at least four dozen small buildings, all very different, dotted around the farmland as vantage points. The interplay between these elements led to the concept of "landscaped garden", which still today is England's most successful export, apart from its language. The Gothic Temple is no longer just for strolling around in. At the end of the nineteen-sixties, the newly founded Landmark Trust converted it into a holiday apartment for four people. Michael and Benjamin Gibbon restored the heraldry ornamentation in the round main hall. Three annexes house all the necessary amenities for a comfortable stay. The interiors exhibit the same values and standards as the outward architecture.

<<< Facts: "I'm glad the Gothic Temple exists, so ordinary people can stay in places as extraordinary as this." Guestbook

Booking information:

Stowe, Buckinghamshire UK

T +44 (0)1628 - 82 59 25

info@landmarktrust.org.uk

bookings@landmarktrust.org.uk

www.landmarktrust.org.uk

Natur/
nature

„Kennen wir uns nicht?" Diese Frage ist hier keine Floskel. Der Gothic Temple und seine Umgebung blitzen in vielen Filmen auf, darunter Blockbustern wie „Indiana Jones – der letzte Kreuzzug" oder „James Bond – die Welt ist nicht genug". Verantwortlich dafür ist die Lage: Das Set liegt auf halbem Weg von London nach Birmingham, und damit für das Gros angelsächsischer Studios quasi vor der Haustür. Überdies lässt die Location an malerischen Motiven nichts zu wünschen übrig.

Der Gothic Temple wurde 1748 von James Gibbs errichtet. Er setzte den Schlussstein an Stowe House, das sich bereits ein Jahrhundert zuvor anschickt, zum kolossalen Schloss aufzusteigen. Das ungleich größere Masterpiece gelingt indes auf den 200 Hektarn drumherum. Hier wirken seit 1718 Charles Bridgeman, William Kent und Lancelot Capability Brown. Die drei Gartenpioniere legen Weiher und Rundwege an. Dazu kommen gut vier Dutzend höchst unterschiedliche Kleinarchitekturen, welche als Point de Vues in das Farmland gestreut werden. Im Zusammenspiel entsteht jene Ausdrucksform, die bis heute Englands erfolgreichsten Exportschlager nach der Sprache selbst darstellt: Der „Landschaftsgarten" ist erfunden!

Dass der Gothic Temple allein dem Lustwandel dient, hat sich inzwischen geändert. Ende der 1960er Jahre funktioniert ihn der gerade gegründete Landmark Trust zur Ferienwohnung für vier Personen um. Michael und Benjamin Gibbon restaurieren den Heraldik-Schmuck des runden Hauptraums. Ihre drei Satelliten nehmen alles auf, was den Aufenthalt angenehm macht. Letztlich stehen die Inneren Werte dem ersten äußeren Eindruck in nichts nach.

<<< Facts: „I'm glad the Gothic Temple exists, so ordinary people can stay in places as extraordinary as this." Gästebuch

★ Grotte della Cività

Via Cività 28 (Sasso Barisano) | I-75100 Matera

Grotte della Città ... Albergo Diffuso ... these names sound obscure, but this residence offers precisely what its names suggest. The grottoes are nestled exactly halfway between the heel and the toe of Italy's boot-like shape. 50 kilometres inland from the Gulf of Taranto, the landscape appears barren and rutted. Mother Nature has little resistance to erosion here. At the same time, it is easy to carve caves out of the adobe, also for the purpose of habitation. This is exactly what happened here in the New Stone Age, so no less than 12,000 years ago! And so they remained as dwellings. It was only in the modern era that it was deemed untenable for human beings to live in caves. Consequently, after the Second World War, replacement buildings were developed. This was not very original, but at least it prevented a mass exodus from the town. Matera—surrounding the Grotte della Città —is still a prospering provincial capital of more than 60,000 inhabitants, unlike the many dwindling towns in central and southern Italy. The grottoes were designated a UNESCO World Heritage site in 1993. It was only after their careful restoration by Sextantio Restauri Italiani that they no longer stood completely empty. In cooperation with David Chipperfield, the company created eighteen holiday residences within the Sasso Barisano cliffs. Furniture and lighting accentuate the sparse and modern interiors, which are typical of the star architect. Today the almost windowless grottoes for two to four people, up to 12 metres deep, appear extremely light. It is only at nighttime that one can picture that dozens of people and their domestic animals once jumped around here in the dark. The obscure acoustics in this Diffuso setting also make it possible to imagine such a civilisation ...

<<< Facts: In cooperation with David Chipperfield, Sextantio Restauri Italiani created eighteen holiday residences within the Sasso Barisano cliffs.

Booking information:

Via Cività 28 (Sasso Barisano)

I-75100 Matera

T +39 0835 / 33 27 44

matera@sextantio.it

www.sextantio.it

Berge/
hills

Natur/
nature

Ferienhaus/
holiday house

Grotte della Cività ... Albergo Diffuso ... die Bezeichnungen klingen obskur – doch diese Unterkunft bietet haargenau das, was ihr Name verspricht. Es beginnt bereits mit der Lage: Im Stiefel, den Italien bildet, verstecken sich die Grotten genau zwischen Hacke und Spitze.

50 Kilometer oberhalb des Golfs von Tarent scheint das Land karg und zerfurcht. Tatsächlich leistet Mutter Erde der Erosion nur wenig Widerstand. Zugleich macht es der Lehmstein ungemein leicht, Höhlen heraus zu schneiden – zum Wohnen zum Beispiel. Genau das geschah hier schon in der Jungsteinzeit, also vor nicht weniger als 12.000 Jahren!

Im Grunde blieb es dabei. Erst der Moderne erschien es unhaltbar, dass Menschen in Höhlen hausen. Also wurde nach dem Zweiten Weltkrieg für Ersatzbauten gesorgt. Das war zwar nicht eben originell, stoppte aber die Stadtflucht. Im Gegensatz zu den vielen aussterbenden Orten Mittel- und Süditaliens ist Matera, das sich auf die Grotte della Cività gründet, nach wie vor eine prosperierende Provinzkapitale. Und inzwischen zählt die Gemeinde sogar mehr als 60.000 Einwohner.

Die Grotten wiederum mochte die UNESCO 1993 zum Weltkulturerbe erheben. An ihrem Leerstand änderte erst die sachte Sanierung durch Sextantio Restauri Italiani etwas: Zusammen mit David Chipperfield richtete die Firma im Berg von Sasso Barisano 18 Feriendomizile ein. Mit Möbel und Leuchten wurden Akzente gesetzt, die so sparsam und modern ausfallen wie in anderen Werken des Stararchitekten. Heute wirken die fast fensterlosen, bis zu 12 Meter tiefen Stollen für zwei bis vier Personen ungeheuer licht. Dass hier früher Dutzende Menschen mitsamt ihren Haustieren durchs Dunkel sprangen, lässt sich erst in der Nacht erahnen. Die obskure Akustik in diesem Diffuso-Setting macht noch jeden Zivilisationszustand glaubhaft ...

<<< Facts: „In einiger Entfernung vom Bahnhof kam ich auf eine Straße, die nur auf einer Seite von alten Häusern gesäumt war und auf der anderen an einem Abgrund entlangführte. In diesem Abgrund lag Matera ..." Carlo Levi: Christus kam nur bis Eboli

★ Havenkraan van Harlingen

Dokkade 5 | NL-8862 NZ Harlingen

Watch out, lads! Here you can pull off a great stunt, while hardly lifting a finger! Your joystick will make 65 tons of steel rotate. All heads will turn immediately towards your shelter for the night!

Those attracted by such a proposition will find themselves in a veritable film set of a location: The Harlingen harbour crane rises to a height of almost 50 metres above ground level. During the last half a century, its job was a rather lonely one: It heaved Russian or Scandinavian wood onto Friesian shores. Since its conversion, after the turn of the millennium, anyone can enjoy its lofty heights.

The ascent is now facilitated by lifts, which look like the unfolding of a science fiction series. The second one, in particular, is like something from Star Trek: the visitor is sucked up into the machine room like tube mail. There the giant mechanism lies in silence, before it is cranked up into action and the noise drowns everything else out. The controls are located, as is typical, in the cockpit on the upper deck, which now also serves as a breakfast terrace. The living space lies between the two, filled with a wild mixture of industrial design from every imaginable era.

However, conditions in the 60-cubic-metre box never seem too cramped, because the bay window magnifies the sense of space a million times. Not only does the sunset shine directly onto the double bed, but if you type onto the touchscreen correctly, you can also magic the first morning rays to shine right onto your pillow.

**<<< Facts: "We'll bet you've never dreamt of that!"
Dromen aan Zee, self-portrait**

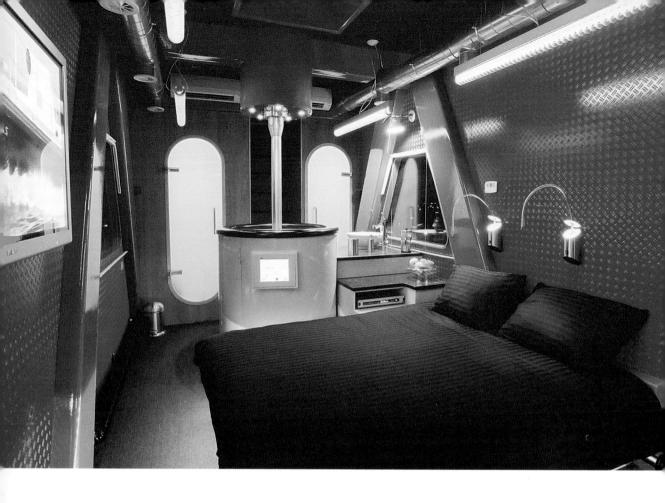

Obacht, Jungs: Hier könnt Ihr das ganz große Ding drehen, ohne kaum mehr als den kleinen Finger krumm zu machen! Euer Joy-Stick bringt 65 Tonnen Stahl zum Rotieren. Augenblicklich nimmt die ganze Welt Kurs auf Euer Nachtlager!

Wer der Verheißung folgt, findet sich an einer wahrhaft filmreifen Location wieder: Fast 50 Meter über Normal-Null trumpft der Hafenkran von Harlingen auf. Während des letzten halben Jahrhunderts mochte sein Metier zumeist ein einsames sein: Er hievte russisches oder skandinavisches Holz auf friesische Gestade. Nach dem Millennium umgebaut, darf heute jeder hoch hinaus. Der Aufstieg vollzieht sich neuerdings mithilfe von Aufzügen, die wie die Evolutionsstufen einer Science-Fiction-Serie daherkommen. Vor allem der zweite ist des Raumschiffs Enterprise würdig: Rohrpostgleich wird der Besucher in die Maschinenhalle gesaugt. Dort blinkt das riesige Getriebe noch still vor sich hin; bald wird man hier sein eigenes Wort nicht mehr verstehen ...

Die Steuerung erfolgt klassischerweise von der Kanzel auf dem Oberdeck, das inzwischen auch Frühstücksterrasse ist. Zwischen beidem liegt der Wohntrakt, welchen eine wilde Mischung von Industriedesign aller erdenklichen Epochen fast voll ausfüllt. Eng geht es in der 60-Kubikmeter-Box allerdings nie zu, weil das Erkerfenster das Millionenfache an Wirkraum hereinholt. So trifft nicht nur der Sonnenuntergang punktgenau das Doppelbett. Wer am Touchscreen richtig tippt, wird den ersten Morgenstrahl genauso punktgenau auf die Kissen zaubern.

**<<< Facts: „Davon haben Sie noch nie geträumt!"
Dromen aan Zee, Selbstdarstellung**

Booking information:

Dokkade 5

NL-8862 NZ Harlingen

T +31 (0)517 / 41 44 10

info@dromenaanzee.nl

www.dromenaanzee.nl

Stadt/
city

Natur/
nature

★ Hotel Brosundet

Apotekergata 5 | NO-6004 Ålesund

Sea and land are two different things, everyone knows that. The quantum leap that actually separates the two spheres will become apparent to every sea voyager steering towards Hotel Brosundet in Ålesund. The little art nouveau town, which was rebuilt after a major fire in 1904, is nestled into the rugged fjords of Norway's west coast. Its harbour peninsular is surrounded by islets. The lighthouse on the quay is scarcely bigger than an advertising column. The fish warehouse next to it has ceiling heights that were classified as "too low" by local housing laws. Nevertheless, both structures were converted into Hotel Brosundet. The lodging opened in 2008, offering no less than 47 guestrooms, which can also be used as work spaces. The Snøhetta designers dug deep into their bag of tricks to create this spatial miracle. The warehouse was gutted as far as possible, some of its windows were carefully enlarged, and the wooden support structure was completely exposed. The brickwork remained bare, as it was, or else was painted once at the most. The rustic interiors feature modern miniature bathrooms, standing in the rooms like aquariums. Such is there visual appeal that it is easy to overlook the fact that storage space is even more limited in the warehouse than it was before. The lighthouse was quite a different matter. Even the bed had to fit into the interior space with a diameter of just three metres. The maisonette, a mere 13 square metres in size, is a lovely cosy nest. Especially when a storm is brewing over the North Atlantic, every guest will be grateful to be on dry land and not out at sea ...

<<< Facts: Snøhetta—meaning "snowcap"—is ambiguous: it refers to a well-known mountain in Norway, as well as to the country's most renowned architecture firm. In 1989, not long after the company was founded, it experienced its first big success story: Snøhetta asserted itself against more than 500 competitors for the rebuilding of the Library of Alexandria. Three decades later, the new Oslo Opera House earned equal recognition. Compared to these milestones, this hotel conversion might seem insignificant, but the first impression is deceptive. The key to appreciating their achievement lies in your own hands, as soon as you open the door with it and cross the threshold.

Meer ist nicht gleich Land, das weiß im Grunde jeder. Welcher Quantensprung beide Sphären tatsächlich trennt, erfährt freilich erst der Seereisende, der das Hotel Brosundet in Ålesund ansteuert. Das Jugendstil-Städtchen, das nach einem Großbrand 1904 auf einen Schlag neu entstand, ist eine Miniatur der zerklüfteten Fjorde an Norwegens Westküste. Seine Hafenhalbinsel sieht sich umringt von Eilanden. Der Leuchtturm am Kai ist kaum größer als eine Litfaßsäule. Der Fischspeicher nebenan bietet Deckenhöhen, die hiesige Beherbergungsgesetze als „zu niedrig" eingestuft hätten.

Und doch wurden beide Häuser für das Hotel Brosundet umgebaut. 2008 eröffnete die Vollpension mit nicht weniger als 47 Fremdenzimmern, die sich sogar noch als Arbeitsplatz andienen. Für dieses Raumwunder griffen die Designer von Snøhetta tief in die Trickkiste. Das Warenlager wurde soweit als möglich ausgeweidet, manch Fenster behutsam vergrößert, das tragende Holzgerippe allseits freigelegt. Der Backstein blieb nackt, wie er war, oder erhielt höchstens einen Anstrich. Zum rustikalen Inventar gesellten sich moderne Mini-Bäder, die aquariumsgleich im Zimmer stehen. Dank dieser Schauwerte lässt sich leicht übersehen, dass Stauraum in dem Lagerhaus nun knapper denn je ist.

Beim Leuchtturm half das alles nichts: Hier muss sich sogar das Bett in die drei Meter Innendurchmesser schmiegen. Mit gerade 13 Quadratmetern ist die Maisonette ein ideales Kuschelnest. Spätestens, wenn der Nordatlantik mal wieder seine stürmische Seite zeigt, ist jeder Gast dankbar, dass Meer und Land so gar nicht mehr dasselbe sind...

<<< Facts: Snøhetta – zu Deutsch „Schneekappe" – ist doppeldeutig: Das Wort bezeichnet einen bekannten Berg Norwegens und zugleich das renommierteste Architekturbüro des Landes. Kaum gegründet gelang ihm 1989 der große Wurf: Bei der Wiedererrichtung der großen Bibliothek von Alexandria obsiegte Snøhetta gegen mehr als 500 Konkurrenten. Nicht weniger Beachtung fand drei Jahrzehnte später das frisch fertiggestellte Opernhaus von Oslo. Im Vergleich zu diesen Meilensteinen mag sich der Hotelumbau von Ålesund unbedeutend ausnehmen, doch entspricht es exakt Snøhettas Planungsansatz: Den Schlüssel zu ihrem Schaffen liefert ein Papierprojekt, das besagten Berg soweit zusammenfaltet, bis er in jede Hand passt ...

Booking information:

Apotekergata 5

NO-6004 Ålesund

T +47 70 11 45 00

post@brosundet.no

www.brosundet.no

Natur/
nature

★ Hüttenpalast Indoor Camping

Hobrechtstraße 66 | D-12047 Berlin

The Hüttenpalast ("Hut Palace") promises glamping for warm shower addicts and city freaks. It is also the right place for visitors to Berlin who want to get to know the creative side of the metropolis.

Then location in itself is quite an experience: just 10 minutes on the subway and the centre of the Mitte district seems like a distant memory. Alexanderplatz gives way to Hermannplatz, which is at the heart of the Neukölln neighbourhood, at the top end of the hip scale. A five-minute walk and you find yourself in a typical Berlin back yard. While the tenement at the front is still in residential use, vacuum cleaners haven't been manufactured in the factory block to the rear for a long time. Its ground floor, framed by a wildly romantic garden café, houses the Hüttenpalast.

Nomen est omen: under the Prussian vaulted ceiling you will find a duplex house ("Valley and Peak Chalet"), the "Old Palace" that is knocked together out of antique furniture, as well as three caravans built in 1958–1976, with the names of "Heartbreaker", "Little Sister" and "Swallow's Nest". The latter were completely gutted by the design networker Yoraco Gonzalez and transformed into little works of art.

Apart from that, the interior of the hall represents a parody of the allotment gardener's paradise. Potted plants and chaotically mixed groups of garden chairs stand under bare birches. Those who consider all of this too basic will also find six highly serious loft rooms under the same roof. Thank you, you are too kind!

<<< Silke Lorenzen grew up in Pakistan, in the Philippines, in China and in India. After an odyssey through Germany, from Hesse to Bavaria, Hamburg and Leipzig, she finally found new roots in Berlin and decided to stay here, even though there were no mangos falling into her lap ...

<<< Sarah Vollmer was born in the nineteen-seventies in West Berlin. Although it's hard to believe, her childhood was spent in a rural idyll. The memories of collecting milk from the farmer behind the hill with the windmill and of steeling corn cobs from the fields reflect her early passion for all things edible ...

Glamping für Warmduscher und Stadtneurotiker verspricht der Hüttenpalast. Man möchte hinzufügen: Berlin-Besucher, welche die Kreativmetropole kennenlernen wollen, sind hier ebenfalls richtig! Das zeigt sich schon bei der Anreise: 10 Minuten U-Bahn-Fahrt machen die Mitte von Mitte fast vergessen. Aus dem Alexander- wird der Hermannplatz. Der ist der Nabel eines Kiezes, dessen Hippness-Skala noch nach oben offen ist: Neukölln. Weitere fünf Minuten Fußweg und wir verirren uns in einen typisch Berliner Hinterhof. Während in der Mietskaserne (Vorderhaus) nach wie vor gewohnt wird, stellt die Stockwerksfabrik hinten längst keine Staubsauger mehr her. Im Erdgeschoss, das von einem wildromantischen Garten-Café gerahmt wird, findet schließlich der Hüttenpalast seinen Platz. Nomen est omen: Unter der preußischen Kappendecke stehen ein Doppelhaus vom Nikolaus („Berg- und Tal-Hütte"), der aus Antik-Möbeln zusammengezimmerte „Alte Palast" sowie drei Wohnwagen der Baujahre 1958–1976, die auf die Namen „Herzensbrecher", „Kleine Schwester" und „Schwalbennest" hören. Letztere hat der Design-Netzwerker Yoraco

Gonzalez komplett entkernt und zu kleinen Kunstwerken hochgerüstet. So trat etwa Kokon aus Holzklamotten an die Stelle des Plaste-Bauchs aus DDR-Zeiten. Ansonsten bietet das Halleninterieur die Parodie eines Laubenpieper-Paradieses: Unter Birkenskeletten stehen Topfblumen und chaotisch durchgemischte Gartenstuhlgruppen. Wem das alles zu verprömmelt ist, der findet nebenan übrigens auch sechs hoch seriöse Loft-Zimmer. Danke, aber dit is zu jütig!

<<< Silke Lorenzen wuchs in Pakistan, auf den Philippinen, in China und Indien auf. Nach einer Deutschland-Odyssee von Hessen über Bayern, Hamburg und Leipzig konnte sie in Berlin endlich neue Wurzeln schlagen und entschied sich zu bleiben, obwohl ihr die Mangos hier nicht mehr in den Schoß fielen ...

<<< Sarah Vollmer erblickte im Westberlin der 70er Jahre das Licht der Welt. Auch wenn das kaum einer glauben mag, war ihre Kindheit von einer ländlichen Idylle geprägt. In den Erinnerungen an das Milchholen beim Bauern hinterm Windmühlenberg und Mais Klauen in den Feldern spiegelt sich ihre frühe Leidenschaft für alles Essbare wider ...

Booking information:

Hobrechtstraße 66

D-12047 Berlin

T +49 (0)30 / 37 30 58 06

F +49 (0)30 / 37 30 57 98

info@huettenpalast.de

www.huettenpalast.de

Stadt/
city

★ Kakslauttanen Arctic Resort

Kiilopääntie 9 | FI-99830 Saariselkä

You're off on a safari! But watch out, make sure you head in the right direction: You're going northwards, to the extreme north, as far as 250 kilometres north of the 66th circle of latitude. Here lies Hotel Kakslauttanen, halfway between the North Cape and the Arctic Circle, at the heart of the land of the midnight sun, beckoning you to join husky and reindeer safaris! The majority of ist lodgings are just as traditional. Around 66 log cabins are dotted around the nearly one-square-kilometre site, including a room that is concealed beneath a metre of turf, aimed mostly at honeymooners. In addition, there are various temporary structures made of snow and ice, including a chapel, an ice bar and igloos, as can also be found elsewhere. Kakslauttanen is in a league of its own when it comes to ist 67 glass igloos, which are only available from rom the end of August until end of April when we have the northern lights season. They are made of glass, rising out of the Lapp tundra. Two beds, a WC and a wardrobe are all that the domes contain. Nothing gets in the way of the view of the northern lights in the sky!

It is dark most of the time. At the beginning of the season the polar night seems endless. Owing to a special coating, the glass is never frosted over. Even snow doesn't get in the way of the views, as there's rarely more than a metre of it. The winter here is as dry as it is cold.

It is a well-known fact that Finns invented the sauna, to counter winter temperatures averaging minus 14 degrees centigrade. Kakslauttanen has the largest in the world, with smoke rather than steam. A Fata Morgana is nothing in comparison!

<<< Facts: "What should I wear to bed in a snow igloo?—Warm underclothes are advisable. In addition, we will provide you with woollen socks and a hat. It's a good idea to get some exercise before you snuggle into your sleeping bag. It also helps to have a snack to boost your energy levels, like chocolate!" FAQ, Kakslauttanen

Heia Safari! Aber Achtung, nur nicht falsch abbiegen: Es geht nach Norden, in den hohen Norden: Erst 250 Kilometer nördlich des 66. Breitenkreises läuft die Anreise langsam aus. Hier, auf halbem Weg zwischen Nordkap und Polarkreis, mitten im Reich der Mitternachtssonne, liegt das Kakslauttanen Arctic Resort und bittet zu Husky- und Rentier-Safaris!

Ähnlich traditionell sind auch die meisten seiner Unterkünfte. Auf dem fast einen Quadratkilometer großen Areal sind gut 66 Blockhütten verstreut: darunter ein Gemach, das unter meterdickem Torf verborgen ist und sich vorrangig an Flitterwöchner wendet. Hinzu kommen allerlei temporäre Bauten wie Kapelle, Eisbar und Iglus, die aus Schnee sind und sich so oder so ähnlich auch anderswo finden lassen.

Außer Konkurrenz steht Kakslauttanen freilich mit seinen 67 modernen Iglus, die zwischen Ende August und April buchbar sind. Vollkommen gläsern ragen sie aus der lappländischen Tundra. Zwei Betten, WC und Kleiderschrank füllen die Kuppeln komplett aus. Nichts verstellt den Blick auf die Polarlichter am Himmel! Dunkel ist es die meiste Zeit, zu Saisonbeginn dauert die Polarnacht gar ewig. Dank Spezialbeschichtung bleiben die Scheiben stets eisblumenfrei. Selbst Schnee kann die Sicht kaum stören, mehr als ein

Meter liegt so gut wie nie. Denn: So kalt die Winter hier sind, so trocken sind sie auch.

Gegen Jahresendzeittemperaturen von im Schnitt etwa 14 Grad unter Null haben Finnen bekanntlich die Sauna erfunden. Kakslauttanen bietet sogar die weltgrößte, die mit Rauch – nicht Dampf – betrieben wird. Eine Fata Morgana ist nichts dagegen!

<<< Facts: „Wie soll man sich im Schneeiglu zum Schlafen anziehen? – Warme Unterwäsche ist empfehlenswert. Zusätzlich bekommen Sie von uns Wollsocken und eine Mütze. Es ist eine gute Idee, sich etwas zu bewegen, bevor Sie in den Schlafsack kriechen. Auch hilft, etwas Kleines zu essen, um Energie zu gewinnen: zum Beispiel Schokolade!" FAQ, Kakslauttanen

Booking information:

Kiilopääntie 9

FI-99830 Saariselkä

T +358 (0)16 / 66 71 00

F +358 (0)16 / 66 71 68

hotel@kakslauttanen.fi

www.kakslauttanen.fi

Natur/
nature

★ Kapari Natural Resort

Kapari Natural Resort Santorini | GR-84700 Imerovigli

Santorini doesn't just look like Mother Nature's womb: the Cycladic archipelago was explosively ejected from it. The group of islands was formed after a devastating volcanic eruption in the sixteenth century BC. After that, the Aegean inhabitants tried to protect Santorini, but the settlers were always cautious, literally clinging on to the edge of the crater. Periodic earthquakes have always lurked beneath the 80 square-kilometre water surface, waiting to take the island by surprise. The last major quake in 1956 was so violent that whole settlements had to be evacuated immediately. Imerovigli, in the middle of the north side of Santorini, was in danger of being reduced to rubble.

Some people refused to be banished for good, such as the Adamidis family. Rena and Takis painstakingly dug their home, which had stood there for a quarter of a millennium, back out of the rubble again. In 2009 their son Philip converted the basements into luxury accommodation, creating a very special experience. Snuggling into his residential caves or diving into the private pool, with the view over nature's womb,

comes very close to the aforementioned feeling of safety and well-being. The best thing of all is that you can decide yourself, to a certain extent, how long you would like to stay and enjoy these feelings for.

<<< Facts: According to legend, the Cycladic archipelago was formed from a clump of earth that the Argonauts threw overboard from their ship. The name originates from the Venetians, who captured the isle at the end of the Middle Ages and dedicated it to St. Irene. The Italian colonial name became so well-established amongst the Greeks that it remained unchanged.

Santorini sieht nicht nur aus wie der Schoß von Mutter Natur. Das Kykladen-Archipel wurde direkterdings von ihm ausgespien: Die Inselgruppe entstand bei einer gewaltigen Vulkaneruption im 16. Jahrhundert vor Christus. Danach mochten die Ägäis-Anrainer Santorini schützen, doch blieben Siedler stets vorsichtig: Sie krallten sich buchstäblich am Kraterrand fest. Denn was unter der 80 Quadratkilometer großen Wasserfläche schlummert, überrascht immer wieder mit Erdbeben. 1956 wirkte der vorerst letzte Stoß so verheerend, dass postwendend Siedlungen offiziell aufgegeben werden sollten. Imerovigli, mittenmang Santorinis Nordseite gelegen, drohte nicht mehr zu sein als eine Schutthalde.

Zu den Menschen, die da nicht mitmachten, zählte die Familie Adamidis: In mühevoller Kleinarbeit gruben Rena und Takis ihr Anwesen, das zuvor ein Vierteljahrtausend überdauert hatte, einfach wieder aus. 2009 verwandelte Sohn Philip die Souterrains dann in eine Luxusherberge. Und was für eine: Sich in seine Wohnhöhle zu kuscheln oder in den Privatpool einzutauchen und immer den Schoß der Natur vor Augen zu haben, kommt der Ur-Geborgenheit extrem nah. Und das allerbeste: Wie lange Sie die Gefühl genießen, bestimmen Sie hier weitgehend selbst!

<<< Der Sage nach entstand das Kykladen-Archipel aus einem Klumpen Erde, den die Argonauten einst von ihrem Schiff warfen. Der Name stammt von den Venezianern, die das Eiland im ausgehenden Mittelalter vereinnahmten und der Heiligen Irene weihten. Die italienische Kolonialbezeichnung bürgerte sich unter den Griechen soweit ein, dass es bei Santorini blieb.

Booking information:

Kapari Natural Resort Santorini

GR-84700 Imerovigli

T +30 (0)22860 / 211 20

F :+30 (0)22860 / 211 19

info@kaparisantorini.gr

www.kaparisantorini.gr

Meer/ ocean   Natur/ nature

★ Kelebek Hotel

Yavuz Sokak 1 | TR-50180 Goreme (Nevsehir)

Sleep like the smurfs. This is a real possibility, owing to the fact that Mother Nature pulled out all the stops all around Goreme. Volcanoes erupted out of the earth. The first wave of eruptions buried central Anatolia under masses of ash. The second wave and tons of lava thickened the ash to tuff. While the soft and porous subsoil had little resistance to erosion, the surface layer stood its ground against desert winds and ice storms. This resulted in magical cliff formations, including hundreds of so-called fairy chimneys, which look just like the smurfs' mushroom houses.

Cave dwellers discovered the landscape and, up until antiquity, their safety instinct drove them ten storeys deep into the ground! Early Christian churches took over the fairy chimneys after that. The cliffs are still inhabited up until today. Summer heat and winter frost are naturally insulated, ensuring a pleasant temperature all year round. All of this was awarded the highest possible distinction by UNESCO in 1985: the National Park of Goreme is both a cultural and a natural heritage site, one of only thirty worldwide.

Since then, the sleepy cliff village has become a stronghold of cave tourism. Of the countless lodgings, which are partly the product of workmanship and partly artefacts, the Kelebek Hotel has the widest range of options. The 31 rooms range from luxury vaulted suites, decorated with archeological finds and with access to private panoramic terraces, to simple shelters right on the peak of the cliff mushrooms. If you sleep up there you really will feel like you're a smurf!

<<< Facts: The Kelebek Hotel is located in the National Park of Goreme that is both a cultural and a natural heritage site by UNESCO.

Schlafen wie die Schlümpfe: Dafür hat Mutter Natur rund um Goreme alle Register gezogen. Vulkane brachen aus dem Boden. Die erste Eruptionswelle begrub Zentral-Anatolien unter Unmengen von Asche. Der zweite Schub verdichtete den Staub durch Tonnen von Lava zu Tuffstein. Während der weich-poröse Untergrund der Erosion wenig entgegenzusetzen hatte, konnten der Deckschicht weder Wüstenwinde noch Eisstürme etwas anhaben. So entstanden märchenhafte Felsformationen, darunter hunderte sogenannter Feenkamine, die den Pilzbehausungen der Schlümpfe wie aus dem Gesicht geschnitten sind. Tatsächlich entdeckten Höhlenmenschen die Landschaft für sich: Bis in die Antike trieb sie ihr Schutzinstinkt zehn Etagen tief in den Untergrund! Danach weideten frühchristliche Kirchen die Feenkamine aus. Noch heute wird in den Felsen, in denen sich Sommerhitze und Winterfrost von selbst in Wohlfühlklima verwandeln, gern gewohnt. Das alles adelte die UNESCO 1985 mit dem höchsten Titel, den die Weltgemeinschaft zu vergeben hat: Der Nationalpark von Goreme repräsentiert sowohl ihr Natur- als auch ihr Kulturerbe! Selbiges können global keine 30 Orte von sich sagen.

Seither hat sich das verschlafene Felsendorf zur Hochburg des Höhlentourismus entwickelt. Von den zahllosen Unterkünften, die halb Werk, halb Artefakt sind, hält das Kelebek Hotel das breiteste Angebot bereit: Die 31 Zimmer reichen von luxuriösen Gewölbesuiten, die sich mit archäologischen Fundstücken und privaten Panoramaterrassen schmücken, bis zu einfachen Nachtlagern, die direkt in der Spitze der Felsenpilze liegen. Keine Frage: Hier zu schlafen, das schlumpft!

<<< Facts: Der Nationalpark von Goreme, in dem sich das Kelebek Hotel befindet, ist UNESCO Natur- und Kulturerbe!

Booking information:

Yavuz Sokak 1

TR-50180 Goreme (Nevsehir)

T +90 (0)384 / 271 25 31

T +90 (0)384 / 271 22 80

F +90 (0)384 / 271 27 63

ali@kelebekhotel.com

www.kelebekhotel.com

Natur/
nature

★ Kolarbyn Eco-Lodge

Skärsjön | SE-73992 Skinnskatteberg

Bleep. My Blackberry's battery is now totally flat, silencing the last sign of modern communications. There are no televisions blaring anywhere. Even the good old fax has no place out here. If you dream of being unreachable, then you've definitively come to the right place!

What would take a great deal of wilful effort anywhere else is a natural state of affairs in Kolarbyn. Two hours' drive west of Stockholm the electricity network is very patchy. Even water pipes have never been laid this far inland. Here water has to be sourced from a spring and heated over an open fire.

The mixed forests of central Sweden are not only an endless source of drinking water and firewood. They also provide food: In the mornings blueberry soup simmers over the campfire and mushroom stew in the evenings. The forest fare sustained the charcoal makers of the past, who worked out here for months on end.

The 12 Eco Lodges of Kolarbyn serve as a reminder of their lifestyle. Each of these wooden shacks has barely enough room for two beds, with a fireplace in between for warmth, assuming the residents know how to light it. It is only in the middle that the shelters are high enough to stand up straight in. The earth-covered board roofs have long since been overrun by vegetation. Therefore in Kolarbyn you can literally hear the grass grow. Who said that nature was silent?

<<< Facts: The 12 Eco Lodges of Kolarbyn serve as a reminder of the lifestyle of the charcoal makers of the past, who worked here.

Pölümm. Der Akku meines Blackberrys meldet sich endgültig ab. Damit ist auch das letzte Signal moderner Kommunikation verstummt. Kein Fernseher plärrt weit und breit. Auch das gute alte Fax hat hier draußen keinen Platz. Wer von Unerreichbarkeit träumt – hier bekommt er sie wirklich frei Haus!

Was anderswo ein Willensakt sein mag, ist Kolarbyn qua Natur gegeben. Zwei Autostunden westlich von Stockholm erweist sich das Stromnetz als einzige Lücke. Auch Leitungen, aus denen warmes Wasser sprudeln könnte, haben sich nie soweit ins Landesinnere vorgegraben. Hier will das Nass aus Quellen geschöpft und über der offenen Flamme erhitzt werden. Dabei erweist sich der Mischwald Mittelschwedens nicht nur als unerschöpfliches Reservoir an Trinkwasser und Feuerholz. Er deckt auch den Esstisch: Morgens dampft die Blaubeer-suppe über'm Lagerfeuer, abends das Pilzragout. Wer mehr will, mag das nötige mitbringen. Doch die Verpflegung des Waldes reichte schon den Köhlern, die sich hier einst über Monate verdungen.

Als Reminiszenz an ihre Lebensweise sind auch die 12 Eco-Lodges von Kalorbyn zu verstehen. Jeder dieser Holzverschläge ist kaum größer als zwei Liegen. Zwischen ihnen wärmt ein Kamin, sofern ihn die Bewohner zu befeuern wissen. Auch hat der Unterstand allein mittig ausreichend Höhe, um aufrecht darin zu stehen.

Die erdbedeckten Bretterdächer sind längst von der Pflanzenwelt überwuchert. Und so kann man in Kolarbyn buchstäblich das Grass wachsen hören. Da sage noch einer, die Natur sei leise.

<<< Idyllisch in Mittelschweden gelegen sind die 12 Eco Lodges. Wer sich hier einmietet, dem sind Ruhe und Abgeschiedenheit garantiert.

Booking information:

Skärsjön

SE-73992 Skinnskatteberg

T +46 (0)70 / 400 70 53

info@kolarbyn.se

www.kolarbyn.se

Familie/
family

Natur/
nature

★ **Kruisherenhotel**

Kruisherengang 19–23 | NL-6211 NW Maastricht

Those who are burdened by a lot of responsibility in their working lives don't just seek amusement on holiday. They want to ease their conscience. From time immemorial, people have sought such refuge in a cloister—which was a source of artistic inspiration in Maastricht.

The Kruisheren Cloister has stood at the heart of the Limburgian metropolis since the fifteenth century. It was built by the Order of the Holy Cross, who were dedicated to the quest for knowledge and helped the poor and the sick. Therefore this brotherhood wasn't quite as missionary as many others at that time, which explains the contemplative ambience of the Gothic complex.

The Kruisheren Kirk finally stopped holding religious services during the French Revolution and the other buildings had been converted into barracks, later into an agricultural college. In the new millen-nium, Camille Oostwegel upgraded the ancient walls to a five-star hotel. The former cloister cells were transformed into 50 rooms, while seven rooms were housed in the former gatekeeper's quarters and three in a new building. The scriptorium was converted into a restaurant, winebar, lounge corners and meeting room. The sea of flowers on the forecourt looks even more colourful through the large choir loft windows. Both the interior and the exterior are feature a number of hip design highlights by the interior architect Henk Vos and the lighting designer Ingo Maurer. It should ease any conscience that the traditional caritas merges so seamlessly with really trendy features.

<<< Camille Oostwegel has been maintaining relationships within the church since opening his hotel business. In order to become independent, he negotiated taking over the country estate from the St. Gerlach municipality in 1979. He learnt about the relationships between buildings and hospitality as the first foreign employee of the French Novotel group.

Wer im Job viel zu verantworten hat, verlangt vom Urlaub nicht allein Zerstreuung. Vielmehr will das Gewissen gestreichelt werden. Ins Kloster zu gehen, mochte sich von alters her als Ausweg anbieten – in Maastricht ist es ein geistesgegenwärtiger Kunstgriff!

Im Zentrum der limburgischen Metropole steht seit dem 15. Jahrhundert das Kruisherenklooster. Der Orden des Heiligen Kreuzes, der es errichtete, kopierte vor allem Wissen, half Armen und Kranken. Damit war diese Bruderschaft nicht halb so missionarisch wie viele andere seinerzeit – was den kontemplativen Grundton des gotischen Komplexes bestens erklärt.

So kam es, dass die Kruisherenkirk ihre Gottesdienste während der Französischen Revolution endgültig einstellte und die übrigen Gebäude zur Kaserne und später zur Landwirtschaftsschule entweiht wurden.

Mit dem Millennium rüstete Camille Oostwegel das urgastliche Gemäuer zum 5-Sterne-Hotel hoch.

50 Zimmer zogen in die ehemaligen Klosterzellen, sieben in die Torwächterwohnung, drei entstanden als Neubau. Das Skriptorium verwandelte sich zu Tagungsstätte, Bar, Restaurant und Lounge.

Durch die wintergartengroßen Chorfenster wirkt das Blumenmeer des Vorplatzes noch mal so bunt. Innen wie außen verteilten Innenarchitekt Henk Vos sowie Lichtkünstler Ingo Maurer jede Menge modischer Design-Highlights. Dass die tradierte Caritas so nahtlos in trendigen Lifestyle übergeht, sollte jedes Gewissen beruhigen.

<<< Kirchenkontakte pflegt Camille Oostwegel solange wie seine Hotellerie. Um sich selbstständig zu machen, handelt er ab 1979 die Übernahme des Landguts der Gemeinde St. Gerlach aus. Die Zusammenhänge von Gebäuden und Gastlichkeit lernte er als erster ausländischer Mitarbeiter der französischen Novotel-Gruppe. Heute führt Oostwegel vier Chateauhotels in und um Maastricht.

Booking information:

Kruisherengang 19–23

NL-6211 NW Maastricht

T +31 (0)43 / 329 20 20

kruiserenhotel@chateauhotels.nl

www.chateauhotels.nl

Stadt/city Hotel/hotel

★ Martello Tower

Aldeburgh, Suffolk UK

It should have gone "Bang!" and prevented an invasion, but the shot fired backwards! However, let's go back to where it all started. We're talking about the year 1812. Half of Europe was at war, either for or against Napoleon. After plans forged in Paris to capture Great Britain became public, the island was seized by fear. A further line of defence against the joint sea fleets of France and Spain was planned immediately: over 100 so-called Martello Towers rose up on the Kent, Essex, Suffolk and Sussex coasts.

The name originates from the Corsican Punta Mortella, whose bastion they were modelled on. Only two decades previously, it had stood fast against bombardment by the Royal Navy. Consequently, the British also went on to build simple round towers made of brick, with walls four metres thick. It was only at the mouth of the Alde river, where the line of fortifications ends 100 kilometres northeast of London, that this apparently wasn't deemed sufficient: Here on the narrow saline strip there are four towers in the form of a clover, forming the largest Martello Tower.

The irony of history is that the water remained the only enemy: The armada never came. Napoleon wore himself out in Russia. Instead, civilians took over the tower, especially since the Landmark Trust installed four tourist beds there. During the restoration in 2002, the civil engineer Dave Tomlinson suspended sailcloth over them. His fabric domes may halt the dripping from the ceiling, but not the intensely reverberating echo, even when two strangers kiss here: "mwuaaah, mwuaah, mwuah ..."

<<< Facts: "We will remember the strange acoustics and the fishermen's lights along the beach." Guestbook

Es hätte „Boow!" machen sollen und eine Invasion verhindern – nur ging der Schuss nach hinten los! Doch der Reihe nach: Wir schreiben das Jahr 1812. Halb Europa befindet sich im Krieg, entweder für oder gegen Napoleon. Nachdem aus Paris Pläne zur Einnahme Großbritanniens publik werden, regiert auf der Insel die Angst. Gegen die geballte Flottenstreitmacht Frankreichs und Spaniens wird postwendend eine weitere Verteidigungslinie entworfen: Aus den Küsten Kents, Essex', Suffolks und Sussex' wachsen über 100 sogenannter Martello Towers.

Als Namenspate fungiert das korsische Punta Mortella, als Blaupause die dortige Bastion. Die hatte keine zwei Dekaden zuvor immerhin dem Beschuss der Royal Navy getrotzt. Also bauen die Briten gleichfalls auf ein simples Backsteinrund mit vier Meter dicken Wänden. Allein an der Flussmündung der Alde, wo die Befestigungslinie 100 Kilometer nordöstlich von London endet, scheint das nicht auszureichen: Hier kulminieren gleich vier Türme in Form eines Kleeblatts. Auf dem schmalen Salinen-streifen entsteht der größte Martello Tower überhaupt.

Ironie der Geschichte: Das Wasser ist der End-gegner, die Armada bleibt aus, Napoleon reibt sich in Russland auf. Stattdessen entern Zivilisten den Turm – umso mehr, nachdem der Landmark Trust darin vier Touristenbetten aufstellt. Bei der Restau-rierung im Jahr 2002 überspannt sie der Bau-ingenieur Dave Tomlinson mit Segeltuch. Seine Textilkuppeln mögen das Tropfen von der Decke unterbinden, nicht aber den enormen Raumhall. So echot es nun, wann immer sich hier zwei Fremde küssen: „Pffff..., pfff..., pff..."

<<< Facts: „We will remember the strange acoustics and the fishermen's lights along the beach." Gästebuch

Booking information:

Aldeburgh, Suffolk UK

T +44 (0)1628 - 82 59 25

info@landmarktrust.org.uk

bookings@landmarktrust.org.uk

www.landmarktrust.org.uk

Stadt/
city

Natur/
nature

★ Pixel Hotel

Spittelwiese 13 | A-4020 Linz

Traditionally guests are shown the whole hotel before choosing their room – but in this case that would mean a veritable sightseeing tour that requires an experienced city scout! The easiest way would be to jump in next to the chambermaid who is doing the rounds with a small car. This is because the Pixel Hotel's accommodation units are strewn all around Linz. It was first established when the Upper Austrian capital was the European Capital of Culture in 2009. In the meantime the architecture initiative set up by Sabine Funk, Richard Steger and Christoph Wiedinger stretches beyond the boundaries of the city: there are no less than 20 kilometres as the crow flies between the various beds!

The newest pixel is to be found in the neighbouring municipality of Enns. Since 1568, a 60-metre-high tower has stood in the oldest Austrian town. A human fire alarm, the so-called "Thurner", was housed there at the time, 71 steps above the ground. His modest accommodation, consisting of a stone table, wooden plank bed and tiled stove, was upgraded into a luxury holiday residence by the Enns avant-garde architect Christoph Haas, including a bathroom with a rainforest shower. Historical scripts reproduced on it glass cube provide information about the history of the tower. This can be felt when its bells make the whole stuccoed vault vibrate.

The oldest pixel, on the other hand, takes you back to recent industrial history. It is anchored in Linz harbour, which was important for the development of Upper Austria. Apart from the obligatory double bed, the tug vessel "Traisen" provides two berths, where evenings feel just like they did when the vessel was launched in 1955.

Of course there is more to the region around Linz than just its ambience. Therefore the Pixel Hotel has come up with a special kind of catering: it provides vouchers for the local cafés, and so the tour of the city can end very traditionally: with Linzer tart

<<< Facts: Further pixels are being developed!

<<< Facts: Weitere Pixel sind in Vorbereitung!

Autor: Hans Wolfgang Hoffmann
Content: Sabine Funk, Jürgen Haller, Bernhard Rihl, Richard Steger,
        Christoph Weidinger

Nach alter Manier lässt sich der Gast erst das ganze Hotel zeigen, bevor er sein Nachtlager wählt – hier steht er damit vor einer veritablen Sightseeing-Tour, welche den versierten Städtescout fordert! Am besten er springt dem Zimmermädchen bei, das seinen Rundgang per Kleinwagen absolviert. Das Pixel Hotel requiriert seine Unterkünfte nämlich aus allerlei ungenutzen Räumlichkeiten in und um Linz. Erstmals eingerichtet wurde es, als die oberösterreichische Hauptstadt 2009 Kulturhauptstadt Europas war. Inzwischen sprengt die Architekteninitiative von Sabine Funk, Richard Steger und Christoph Weidinger die Stadtgrenzen: Die einzelnen Betten trennen heute nicht weniger als 20 Kilometer Luftlinie! Das neueste Pixel befindet sich bereits in der Nachbargemeinde Enns. An der ersten Adresse der ältesten Stadt Österreichs erhebt sich seit 1568 der knapp 60 Meter hohe Stadtturm. 71 Stufen über dem Trottoir hauste seinerzeit ein menschlicher Feuermelder, der sogenannte „Turmwärter". Dessen bescheidene Behausung aus Steintisch, Holzpritsche und Kachelofen hat der Ennser Avantgarde-Architekt Christoph Haas zu einem luxuriösen Feriendomizil hochgerüstet, zu dem auch ein Bad mit Regendusche gehört. Historische Schriften, welche auf deren Glaskubus reproduziert sind, geben Auskunft über die Vergangenheit des Turms – wahrhaft spürbar wird sie, wenn das Läutwerk seiner Uhr das ganze Stuckgewölbe zum Vibrieren bringt. In die jüngere Industriegeschichte entführt dagegen das älteste Pixel. Es liegt an der im Linzer Hafen vor Anker, der die Oberösterreich groß gemacht hat. Das Zugschiff „Traisen" bietet neben dem obligaten Doppelbett auch zwei Kojen, in denen sich der Feierabend noch genauso anfühlt wie beim Stapellauf 1955. Natürlich lässt sich die Region um Linz nicht allein über das Ambiente abhandeln. Daher hat sich das Pixel Hotel auch eine besondere Verpflegung ausgedacht: Es stellt Gutscheine für die lokalen Kaffeehäuser. So vermag die Städtetour ganz traditionell ausklingen: mit Linzer Torte!

Booking information:

Spittelwiese 13

A-4020 Linz

T +43 (0)650 / 743 79 53

office@pixelhotel.at

www.pixelhotel.at

Stadt/
city

★ Propeller Island City Lodge

Albrecht-Achilles-Straße 58 | D-10709 Berlin

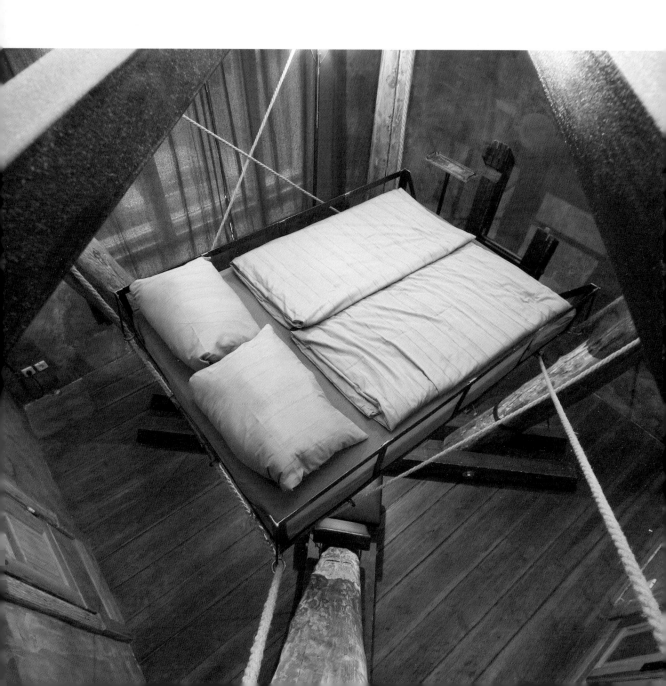

So you think you're familiar with art hotels? Forget all those surrogates. If you really want to stay in a work of art, come to Propeller Island. That's the name of the City Lodge designed by Lars Stroschen, which was actually born out of necessity. In order to finance his own sound studio, the Berlin musician sublet his apartment. It was such a success that self-expression turned into a long-term project: Stroschen took over a guesthouse with several floors, one of many all around Kurfürstendamm, and converted half the building himself over a period of five years.

As a result, each of the 30 rooms is unique: the "Mirror Room" is literally kaleidoscopic, in the "Crypt" you can sleep in a closed coffin. "Freedom" is the name of a prison cell, whose window is only accessible through a breach in the wall. In "Two Lions", the guest can carry out wild animal acts like in the circus, even in front of spectators, as long as the curtain is open. Pars pro toto, the "Gallery" is a lesson in seeing, with its rotating sleeping berth surrounded by empty picture frames. If you look closer, you will find masses of quirky details: furniture standing upside down on the ceiling, or a bed taking off from a launch pad. Baths are made of a plastic sack, grandma's chest of drawers or a pub barrel.

So much creativity is bound to lead to ideas that are not quite so successful. A night in the "Museum" is quite nightmarish. A current example is the suspended bed in "4 Beams", which is a no-no for heavy guests, who weigh more than 300 kg, as otherwise all the cords rip. However, that's to be expected with art ...

<<< Facts: Nomen est omen. The name "Propeller Island" comes from a novel by Jules Verne. In the story, musicians are stranded on an artificial island, which they ultimately take over. Lars Stroschen chose this pseudonym long before he started living according to the story!

Sie glauben, Sie kennen Kunsthotels? Vergessen Sie diese Surrogate. Wer wirklich in einem Gesamtkunstwerk hausen will, zieht nach Propeller Island. So heißt die City Lodge von Lars Stroschen, die eigentlich aus der Not heraus geboren ist: Um sich ein Tonstudio zu finanzieren, gab der Berliner Musiker seine Wohnung zur Untervermietung frei. Doch der Erfolg ließ die Selbstverwirklichung zum Langzeitprojekt werden: Stroschen übernahm eine Etagenpension, wie es rund um den Kurfürstendamm viele gibt, und baute eigenhändig das halbe Haus um. Fünf Jahre dauerte das. Im Ergebnis ist jedes der rund 30 Zimmer ein Unikat: „Mirror Room" versetzt buchstäblich in ein Kaleidoskop, die „Gruft" bietet Schlaf im geschlossenen Sarg. „Freedom" nennt sich eine Gefängniszelle, aus der erst ein Durchbruch in der Wand zum Fenster führt. In „Two Lions" vollführt der Gast Raubtiernummern wie im Zirkus – sofern sich der Vorhang hebt – sogar vor Publikum. Pars pro toto steht die „Gallery": Sie erweist sich - dank rotierender, von leeren Bilderrahmen flankierter Schlafstatt – als Schule des Sehens. Wer genauer hinschaut, findet aberwitzige Details en masse: Mal stehen die Möbel kopfüber auf der Decke, mal hebt das Bett von einer Startrampe ab. Bäder bestehen aus Plastiksack, Omas Kommode oder Kneipenfass. Bei soviel Schöpfergeist bleiben Fehlversuche nicht aus: Die Nacht im „Museum" versammelt diese Alpträume. Ein aktuelles Beispiel liefert das Hängebett von „4Beams", das für Schwergewichte tabu ist, die mehr als 300 kg wiegen, weil sonst alle Stricke reißen. Aber so ist das eben mit der Kunst ...

<<< **Facts: Nomen est omen. Bei „Propeller Island" handelt es sich ursprünglich um einen Roman von Jules Verne. Die Geschichte verschlägt Musiker auf eine künstliche Insel, die sie schließlich übernehmen. Lars Stroschen wählte dieses Pseudonym, lange bevor er begann, die Handlung nachzuleben!**

Booking information:

Albrecht-Achilles-Straße 58

D-10709 Berlin

T +49 (0)30 / 891 90 16

www.propeller-island.com

Stadt/
city

★ Railholiday

Haparanda Station | UK-PL12 5LU St Germans (Cornwall)

Broadly speaking, humanity is divided into two camps: those who play with railways, and those who are played with by railways! The railway enthusiast's paradise lies around 400 kilometres west of London, forms the southern tip of England and is called Cornwall. Land's End may be of general interest to tourists, but only since they heard about it after the development of the railroad. In any case, that's David and Lizzy Stroud's credo, forming the basis of their holiday concept that already encompasses half of the peninsular: Railholiday.

The first Railholiday destination is St Germans, home to 600 souls. A luggage wagon right by the platform, as well as a post wagon, provide self-catering accommodation for two and six people respectively. As the wagons were removed from service at the end of the nineteenth century, they both had to be extensively refurbished. The Strouds rose to the challenge, without any conservative authorities watching over them, as a do-it-yourself project: quite an achievement and to striking effect. The harbour town of Hayle, the Strouds' second stop, is an hour and a half away by train. In addition, Railholiday can recommend a good two dozen day trips. True rail fans will also enjoy the main journey by train: leaving Paddington station at 23.45 and arriving just in time for the first freshly baked roll. Continental tourists always get a city tour into the bargain, thanks to the necessary change of station in London. Everything else challenges either punctuality or the philosophy of the rail enthusiast ...

<<< Facts: The train station is even older than the two wagons at St Germans, extending out of a 30-metre-long viaduct. The structure, by the engineering pioneer Isambard Kingdom Brunel, was inaugurated in 1858, along with the Cornwall Railway. Today the founders of Railholiday live in the station that is considered the best preserved along this stretch.

Die Menschheit teilt sich, ganz grob, in zwei Lager: Diejenigen, die mit der Eisenbahn spielen, und die anderen, mit denen die Eisenbahn spielt! Das Paradies der Pufferküsser liegt 400 Kilometer westlich von London, bildet die Südspitze Englands und nennt sich Cornwall. Das Land's End mag zwar allgemein das Interesse von Touristen finden, das allerdings erst, nachdem sie durch die Bahn davon erfahren konnten. Das ist jedenfalls das Credo von David und Lizzy Stroud, die damit ein Ferienreich begründeten, das bereits die halbe Halbinsel umspannt: Railholiday.

Unter den Destinationen von Railholiday ist das 600-Seelen-Nest St Germans die naheliegendste. Direkt am Bahnsteig bieten ein Gepäckwagen sowie ein Reise-Postamt Schlafplätze zur Selbstverpflegung für zwei bzw. sechs Personen. Nachdem beide Waggons seit dem ausgehenden 19. Jahrhundert Dienst getan hatten, war dafür eine Grundüberholung nötig. Diese stemmten die Strouds ohne jede konservative Autorität im Rücken, im Do-It-Yourself-Verfahren.

Die Hafenstadt Hayle, die zweite Station der Strouds, erreicht der Zug in anderthalb Stunden. Darüber hinaus vermittelt Railholiday gut zwei Dutzend Tagestrips. Richtige Railies werden überdies die Hauptreise per Bahn genießen: Ab 23:45 Paddington bringt einfaches Umsteigen und erreicht just das erste Bäckerbrötchen. Kontinentaltouristen bekommen – dank des Bahnhofswechsels, der in London fällig wird, – immer auch eine Stadtrundfahrt. Alles Weitere stellt entweder die Pünktlichkeit extrem auf die Probe oder die Pufferküsser-Philosophie …

<<< Facts: Noch älter als die beiden Waggons von St Germans ist der Bahnhof, der aus einem gut 30 Meter tiefen Viadukt herauswächst. Das Werk des Ingenieurpioniers Isambard Kingdom Brunel wurde 1858 zusammen mit dem Cornwall Railway eingeweiht.

Booking information:

Haparanda Station

UK-PL12 5LU St Germans (Cornwall)

T +44 (0)1503 / 23 07 83

DaveandLizzy@railholiday.co.uk

www.railholiday.co.uk

Natur/
nature

★ Reddingsboot

Noorderhaven 86 | NL-8861 AR Harlingen

Lilla Marras is at the ready, she has waited long enough. Seconds after the emergency call her rump is already rotating. She ploughs through the turbulent waves with the power of 140 horses. She will not be deterred by anything that the skies may throw at her.

After leaving the production line at Groves & Guttridge in 1955, Lilla Marras was deployed more than a hundred times. She mostly headed north from the Isle of Wight. She is a hero for at least 45 people, who owe her their lives.

Lilla Marras continued to prove her worth. Even after more than 45 years in service, she wasn't condemned to retirement. Instead she changed sides: from the British Atlantic coast to the Dutch North Sea. She found a new home in Harlingen harbour. That's where Lilla Marras met Willem Koornstra. The restorer thoroughly rejuvenated the elderly lady.

Her belly, which had heaved up so many relieved little heaps of misery, underwent fresh cell therapy. The tête-à-tête was consolidated with a two-seater bath made of wood. The liaison culminated with the creation of an unusual double bed in the shape of a waterlily. As before, Lilla Marras still spends most of her time waiting. Her mission hasn't changed significantly either. Instead of rescuing people from distress at sea, she rescues people from their daily grind. Those who are in danger of breaking down at their grindstone can send SOS signals – Lille Marras is there!

<<< Facts: "Thank you, Martjan, my saviour! Could there possibly be a more romantic place for proposing?! My answer was, of course: ay ay, capt'n."
Tanja from Boxtel, in the Lilla Marras logbook

Lilla Marras ist auf dem Posten, sie hat lange genug gewartet. Sekunden, nachdem der Notruf kommt, rotiert es in ihrem Rumpf. Mit der Kraft von etwa 140 Pferden pflügt sie durch den Wellensturm. Nichts, was über ihren Köpfen zusammenschlägt, kann ihr etwas anhaben. Mehr als hundert Mal ist Lilla Marras schon aufgebrochen, seit sie 1955 bei Groves & Guttridge vom Stapel lief. Von der Isle of Wight zog es sie zumeist nach Norden. Für mindestens 45 Menschen ist sie ein Held: Sie verdanken ihr das Leben.

Mitunter zeigt Lilla Marras immer noch, was sie kann. Auch nach über 45 Dienstjahren beschränkt sie sich nicht aufs Altenteil. Vielmehr wechselte sie die Seite: Von der britischen Atlantikküste ging es in die niederländische Nordsee. In Harlingen fand sie ihren neuen Heimathafen. Dort traf Lilla Marras Willem Koornstra. Der Restaurator revitalisierte die Rentnerin

regelrecht. Ihrem Bauch, der so viele erleichterte Häufchen Elend ausgespuckt hatte, verordnete er eine Frischzellenkur. Das Tête-à-tête verstetigte sich in einer zweisitzigen Badewanne aus Holz. Am Ende der Liaison stand schließlich das aparte Doppelbett in Form einer Wasserlilie.

Nach wie vor verbringt Lilla Marras die meiste Zeit mit Warten. Auch an ihrer Mission hat sich nur wenig geändert: Statt aus Seenot errettet sie nun Menschen aus dem Alltagstrott. Wer immer in seiner Tretmühle zusammenzubrechen droht, mag SOS-Signale senden – Lilla Marras ist da!

<<< Facts: „Merci, Martjan, mein Retter! Gibt es einen romantischeren Ort für einen Heiratsantrag?! Meine Reaktion war natürlich: Eye, eye, Capt'n"
Tanja aus Boxtel im Logbuch der Lilla Marras.

Booking information:

Noorderhaven 86

NL-8861 AR Harlingen

T +31 (0)517 / 41 44 10

info@dromenaanzee.nl

www.dromenaanzee.nl

Meer/   Natur/
ocean   nature

★ Roulotte Retreat

UK-TD6 Melrose

Those who are constantly on the road for their job know the feeling of being uprooted. Nobody will find a suitable refuge in New York or Singapore, as even the trendiest globalised metropolis just doesn't do the trick. Of course there is nowhere better for switching off than in the countryside. In Scotland, for example. Even just an hour's drive away from Edinburgh, the hills already put you in a mellow mood. The real consolation is located in a wildflower meadow around the lochan of Roulotte Retreat, just below the legendary Eildon Hills and nearby River Tweed. Here you can hire those rolling refuges that have been used for centuries by travelling folk in eternal exiles which have been created especially for life in Scotland, based on traditional French designs.

Roulotte Retreat is utterly unique having the only collection of hand carved roulottes in UK created by French Artisans. Five years in planning and creating, the circle is now complete with seven roulottes on site in the Scottish Borders countryside. This vision was the dream and now reality of Avril Berry and Alan Fraser, who also have their own therapy businesses in Scotland. There is also Horseshoe Cottage, converted from original Stables with Ruby the Bowtop, an authentic 90 year old Gypsy living wagon in the woodland garden. The interiors, in particular, show that these palaces on wheels are not just a passing whim for the owners. Roulotte Retreat oozes loving attention to detail, lamp tassels and all! The roulottes have their own character and ambience with names like Devanna, Karlotta, Shivanni and Zenaya and are now all settled around the meadow, as though they have always been there. For group celebrations, boutique weddings and workshops there is also a 1950's Studio available for hire, complete with covered deck around a Scots Pine tree which is festooned with solar fairy lights. Inside the Studio is a beautiful light-filled space complete with wood burning stove at its heart, chandeliers and Moroccan lanterns.

<<< Facts: Free Yoga classes on Tuesdays for Roulotte Retreat Guests.

Wer vom Job ständig an immer neue Adressen verschlagen wird, kennt die Empfindung: sich entwurzelt zu fühlen. Niemand wird dann in New York oder Singapur Schutz suchen, denn auch die hippste Globalisierungsmetropole bietet keine Hilfestellung. Viel besser abschalten lässt sich – natürlich – auf dem Land.

In Schottland, zum Beispiel: Seine Hügel stimmen schon eine gute Autostunde vor Edinburgh milde. Der wahre Trost findet sich auf den saftigen Wiesen von Bowden Mill House: Roulotte Retreat. Vermietet werden hier jene rollenden Fluchtburgen, mit denen sich fahrendes Volk seit gut 1.000 Jahren durch's ewige Exil schlägt.

Mit einer solchen abenteuerlichen Unterkunft mögen sich in jüngster Zeit immer mehr Landherbergen schmücken. Hier stehen schon sieben, in Auftrag gegeben von Avril Berry und Alan Fraser, die hauptamtlich als Therapeuten tätig sind. Dass die beiden Besitzer mehr tun, als einen Spleen zu pflegen, verraten insbesondere die Interieurs. Detailliebe tropft Roulotte Retreat aus jeder Pore, weder Kaminpfanne noch Lampenquaste fehlen! Neben der Erbauung halten die Zirkuswagen auch noch eine Erkenntnis bereit: Was als Notbehausung begonnen haben mochte, hat sich zu einem Stück Heimat gemausert. Tja, und wenn schon eine frühere Globalisierungsetappe zu einer solchen Zivilisationsleistung fähig war, sollte es ihr die gegenwärtige doch wohl gleichtun können? Da macht sich der Gast doch gleich wieder gern ans Werk ...

<<< Facts: Auch Wellness-Angebote gibt es für Roulotte-Retreat-Gäste: Jeden Dienstag zum Beispiel stehen hier kostenlose Yogakurse auf dem Programm.

Booking information:

UK-TD6 Melrose

+44 (0)845 / 094 97 29

info@roulotteretreat.com

www.roulotteretreat.com

Natur/
nature

★ Sala Silvergruva

Drottning Christinas Väg | SE-733 36 Sala

Candlelight flickers on natural stone walls, the small lantern only just about lights up the generous double bed. The tuxedo and the little black dress have already been tossed over the leather armchair. It could become the proverbial night before the morning after, but there's just one thing that doesn't fit into the cliché: there are protective helmets lying on the wardrobe! They are a standard precautionary measure, because there are over 150 metres of Dolomite, Calcite and Serpentine piled up over the guests' heads. The pit suite in the Sala mine is the deepest hotel room in the world! This experience is gaining depth all the time. At the entrance, a museum explains what awaits you un-expectedly after a two-hour drive into the forests to the north-west of Stockholm: The Sala silver mine is the country's most significant silver mine. Even Gustav, the first Vasa king, recognised it in his time as the "treasure chamber of the Swedish Empire", some 500 years ago!

Next you take your chance and make the descent down from the shaft tower. After a banquet in the mine hall, the size of a church nave, you are led through the winding labyrinth of tunnels. There you come across magically illuminated underground lakes, which you can even explore with a dive! Finally the staff withdraw discreetly, leaving a midnight snack and a radio device for ordering breakfast, before you are ultimately thrust into the mountain's womb.

<<< Facts: Those who wish to seal their relationship with a ring can scrape together the last specks here: the mine has already delivered 500 tons of silver.

Kerzen flackern über Natursteinwände, gerade so erhellt der kleine Leuchter das generöse Doppelbett gerade so. Smoking und Kleines Schwarzes sind schon über die Ledersessel geworfen. Es könnte der klassische Abend vor dem Morgen danach werden – nur eines passt nicht ins Klischee: Auf der Garderobe liegen Schutz-helme! Sie sind schlichte Vorsichtsmaßnahme. Denn hier werfen sich weit über 150 Meter Dolomit, Kalzit und Serpentin über den Gästen auf. Die Grubensuite des Bergwerks von Sala ist übrigens das tiefste Hotel-zimmer der Welt! Tatsächlich gewinnt dieser Trip stetig an Tiefgang. Als Entree erklärt ein Museum, womit nach zweistündiger Autofahrt in die Wälder nordwestlich von Stockholm kaum zu rechnen war: Das Bergwerk von Sala ist landesweit die bedeutendste Silbermine Schwedens. Schon Gustav, der erste Wasa-König, erkannte in ihr die „Schatzkammer des schwedischen Reiches". Und das war vor 500 Jahren!

Danach heißt es „Glück auf" und vom Förderturm abgeseilt. Auf das Bankett im kirchenschiffgroßen Bergsaal folgt die Führung durch das verwinkelte Stollenlabyrinth. Dort finden sich – magisch erleuchtet – unterirdische Seen, die sich sogar per Tauchgang erkunden lassen!

Schließlich zieht sich das Personal diskret zurück. Für den ultimativen Vorstoß in den Schoß des Berges bleibt ein Mitternachtshappen sowie das Funkgerät, mit dem das Frühstück geordert wird.

<<< Facts: Wer seine Beziehung dermaßen vertieft hat, mag sie per Ring besiegeln wollen. Dafür lassen sich hier die letzten Krumen zusammenkratzen: 500 Tonnen Silber hat das Bergwerk ja bereits zu Tage gefördert ...

Booking information:

Drottning Christinas Väg

SE-733 36 Sala

T +46 (0)224 / 67 72 50 , -6(

info@salasilvergruva.se

www.salasilvergruva.se

Natur/
nature

★ Saljoet

NL-Fryslân

"Clunk!" It's only a brief, metallic sound, but after that you are in quite a different world! As soon as the entrance hatch has snapped shut, all that remains of the Frisian idyll is the view through the portholes. The wide expanse of meadows is gone, as well as the wind that turns the windmills all around.

Everything inside is carefully measured out: table, cupboard, WC ... The sink unit is also the washbasin. Of course the narrow space is very cosy and provides a safe shelter. If the breeze becomes a hurricane, guests will nevertheless breathe still air. Even if the whole shelter was ripped from its mooring and was in danger of being squashed by the sluice gates, the residents could sleep on undisturbed.

For we are in the Saljoet. The name is rather deceptive: In reality, the name of the early Russian space stations refers to a Californian construction. It was built in 1972, to withstand the inferno of exploding oil rigs. After being in service for around 30 years, the gentlemen Veldhuis and Terpstra dragged the Saljoet out of the North Sea and converted it into an accommodation unit for two. Nevertheless: It remains a true rescue capsule. The waves beating against its rump convey a sense of lurking danger. The air is stuffy after a night in the Saljoet. It's good that the morning sun warms the wooden railings. When having breakfast, guests can paddle their feet in the canal and swish their legs through the reeds. The Frisian nightmares evaporate here, leaving a sense of safety and well-being, thanks to the Saljoet ...

<<< Facts: Only the best places in the Friesland, and always near a camping, are good enough, with a total guarantee of tranquillity, peace and panoramas.At the moment, the Saljoet is floating around in the middle of the Friesland waterscape between the typical Friesland villages of Tirns and Sneek.
Peace and Space Guaranteed.

„Klonnk!" Es ist nur ein kurzer, metallischer Laut, doch die Welt danach eine völlig andere! Kaum dass die Einstiegsluke ins Schloss fällt, bleibt von der Idylle Frieslands nur mehr ein Bullaugen-Panorama: Weg ist die Weite der endlosen Wiesen ringsum, verflogen der Wind, der die Mühlen ringsum rotieren lässt, verflogen.

Alles drinnen ist abgezirkelt: Tisch, Schrank, WC ... Die Spüle dient zugleich als Waschbecken. Sicher, auch auf engstem Raum geht es wohnlich zu – doch vor allen Dingen: sicher! Würde die Brise zum Orkan, atmeten die Gäste trotzdem gut abgestandene Luft. Selbst wenn die ganze Behausung sich aus der Vertäuung reißen sollte und von Schleusentoren zerdrückt zu werden drohte – die Bewohner dürfen seelenruhig weiterschlafen.

Denn wir sind im Saljoet. Die Bezeichnung ist eine kleine Lüge: Der Name der frühen russischen Raum-stationen verbirgt in Wahrheit eine kalifornische Konstruktion. Gebaut wurde sie 1972, um das Inferno explodierender Bohrinseln zu überstehen. Nach rund

30 Dienstjahren haben die Herren Veldhuis und Terpstra das Soljoet aus der Nordsee verschleppt und in eine Frischzelle für zwei verwandelt.

Dennoch: Es bleibt eine richtige Rettungskapsel. Die dumpf gegen den Rumpf schlagenden Wellen ver-mitteln das Gefühl ferner Gefahr. Und stickig ist es nach der Nacht im Saljoet sowieso. Wie gut, dass die Morgensonne die hölzerne Reling anwärmt. Bereits beim Frühstück baumeln die Beine im Kanal, streichen die Füße durch's Schilf. Die Albträume Frieslands lösen sich in Wohlgefallen auf. Das Saljoet hat dann ganze Arbeit geleistet ...

<<< Facts: Ruhe, Abgeschiedenheit und ein einmaliges Panorama, all das ist in Friesland garantiert. Zurzeit treibt die Saljoet mitten auf dem friesischen Flachland, umgeben von den typischen pittoresken Dörfern.

Booking information:

NL-Fryslân

T +31 (0)6 / 53 29 96 22

info@saljoet.nl

www.saljoet.nl

Natur/
nature

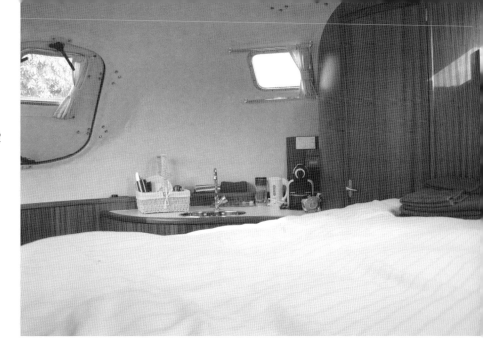

★ Salt & Sill

Koholmen, Strandgatan | SE-471 51 Klädesholmen

Can you still remember Carl Fredricksen? His paradise was a waterfall on the other side of the world. He was thoroughly fed up with the metropolis that he actually lived in. In the end he drifted off into a sea of clouds with his little wooden house attached to thousands of balloons ... at least this is how it was in Pixar's 3-D animation "Up". Salt & Sill converts this film adventure into reality!

The setting is the west coast of Sweden, more precisely the small island of Klädesholmen 70 kilometres north of Göteborg. The island has long since been so overrun with holiday homes that there's hardly room for any more. Consequently, the Hermansson couple fled to the water with Salt & Sill in 2008. As an extension of their resort, the architectural office Mats & Arne designed Sweden's first floating hotel. Standing on a pontoon, there are six two-storey terraced houses, whose interior design is as modern as it is typically Scandinavian. All 23 rooms open out onto terraces, including on the roof, where there is also a pool for guests staying on the upper floor.

Those down below have direct access to the Baltic Sea. The complex was built by the shipyard SF Marina, from where the hotel was shipped to Klädesholmen.

<<< Facts: While the majority of residential boats rarely leave their mooring, Salt & Sill regularly takes to the sea, with its own auxiliary boat SS Silla. The approximately twelve by six metre longboat houses the sauna, the conference venue and the hotel's bridal suite. Two diesel motors propel the catamaran up to 30 km/h. Its horsepower of up to 320 makes Salt & Sill the fastest spa the world has ever seen!

Erinnern Sie sich noch an Carl Fredricksen? Sein Paradies war ein Wasserfall am anderen Ende der Welt. Die Metropole, in der er wirklich wohnte, hatte er gründlich satt. Schließlich entschwebte er mitsamt seinem Holzhäuschen und Abertausenden von Ballons ins Wolkenmeer ... So zu sehen jedenfalls in Pixars 3-D-Animation „Oben". Salt & Sill dreht ebendieses Filmabenteuer um 90 Grad – ins wahre Leben! Schauplatz ist hier die Westküste Schwedens, genauer gesagt die kleine Insel Klädesholmen 70 Kilometer nördlich von Göteborg. Ferienhäuser haben das Eiland längst soweit überwuchert, dass für weitere kaum mehr Platz ist. Prompt flüchtete das Ehepaar Hermansson 2008 mit Salt & Sill aufs Wasser. Als Erweiterung ihres Resorts plante das Architekturbüro Mats & Arne Schwedens erstes schwimmendes Hotel. Sechs zweistöckige Reihenhäuser besetzen einen Ponton mit ebenso modernem wie typisch skandinavischem Wohndesign. Alle 23 Zimmer grenzen an Terrassen, die sich noch auf dem Dach fortsetzen. Für die oberen findet sich dort ein Pool, die unteren verfügen über direkten Zugang zur Ostsee. Die Realisierung übernahm die Werft SF Marina, von der aus das Hotel in toto nach Klädesholmen, zum heutigen Standpunkt verschifft wurde.

<<< Facts: Während die meisten Wohnboote ihren Ankerplatz nur höchst selten verlassen, sticht Salt & Sill regelmäßig in See: mit dem Haussatelliten SS Silla. Das etwa zwölf auf sechs Meter große Beiboot birgt die Sauna, den Tagungstrakt sowie die Hochzeitssuite des Hotels. Zwei Dieselmotoren beschleunigen den Katamaran auf bis zu 30 Km/h: Die Stärke von 320 Pferden verwandelt Salt & Sill zum schnellsten Spa, das die Welt je gesehen hat!

Booking information:

Koholmen, Strandgatan

SE-471 51 Klädesholmen

T +46 (0)304 / 67 34 80

info@saltosill.se

www.saltosill.se

Natur/
nature

Familie/
family

★ Santo Stefano

Via Principe Umberto | I-67020 Santo Stefano di Sessanio

The wind is whistling over the mountain ridge. Apart from a couple of shrubs, there is hardly any vegetation here. Christian Slater and Sean Connery hurry on ... This is the opening scene of Jean-Jacques Annaud's film version of "The Name of the Rose". This preamble would also befit Santo Stefano. The setting is the same: the Middle Ages. Mentioned for the first time around 720, most of the buildings that still crowd within the town walls today were built by the fifteenth century. Like Annaud's opening film set, Santo Stefano lies in the Abruzzo province of L'Aquila, at the heart of the national park of Gran Sasso e Monti della Laga. From the nearest port in Pescara, it is more than an hour's drive inland and uphill, up to an altitude of 1,250 metres above the Adriatic. It is a true hermitage. Over the course of the last century, the number of inhabitants shrank to less than a tenth. Santo Stefano was faced with the same fate of extinction that threatens 15,000 communities in Italy. Sextantio Restauri Italiani mobilised all the funds available to them for the restoration work. The deserted houses are now occupied by an Albergo Diffuso, whose

30 rooms are spread across half of the town centre. The interior fabrics were supplied by local weavers. Local musicians dominate the cultural programme. The businesses that moved into six of the shops also have a "regional" bias.

Thanks to helping themselves, the population is now very stable once again. Furthermore, the community is now officially one of the "most beautiful Italian villages". Thus everything at Santo Stefano points to a happy end, unlike in the aforementioned film!

<<<Facts: Architecture Biennale 2012: If Sextantio Restauri Italiani had restored a country estate in Tuscany or a residence in Rome, it is unlikely that anybody would have taken much notice. This type of thorough renovation has been carried out for decades with regard to such sites. However, to revitalise a whole village using the same methods is innovative and politically relevant. Consequently, Sextantio Restauri Italiani was invited to exhibit their work at the most recent Architecture Biennale. Santo Stefano represented the whole of Italy at the international architecture exhibition.

Über den Bergrücken pfeift der Wind. Außer ein paar kleinen Sträuchern erhebt sich hier kaum etwas. Christian Slater und Sean Connery machen, dass sie weiterkommen ... So beginnt Jean-Jacques Annauds Romanverfilmung „Der Name der Rose". Der Vorspann hätte auch Santo Stefano gut angestanden. Der Schauplatz ist der gleiche: das Mittelalter.

Um 720 erstmals urkundlich erwähnt, standen im 15. Jahrhundert die meisten Bauten, welche die Stadtmauern noch heute ausfüllen. Wie Annauds Einstiegsset liegt Santo Stefano in der Abruzzen-Provinz L'Aquila, mitten im Nationalpark Gran Sasso e Monti della Laga. Vom nächsten Hafen in Pescara fahren Autos über eine Stunde stetig landeinwärts und bergan: bis auf 1.250 Meter über der Adria. Auch die Einsiedelei ist höchst real. Im letzten Jahrhundert fiel die Einwohnerzahl auf weniger als ein Zehntel. Santo Stefano drohte dasselbe Schicksal, das für 15.000 Gemeinden in Italien kaum mehr zu verhindern ist: Aussterben.

Zur Sanierung mobilisierte Sextantio Restauri Italiani die letzten Reserven: In die verwaisten Häuser zog ein Albergo Diffuso, dessen 30 Zimmer sich über den halben Stadtkern verteilen. Die Raumtextilien lieferten lokale Weber; lokale Musiker bestimmen das Kulturprogramm. Und auch für die Gewerke, die sich in sechs Ladenlokalen einrichteten, ist das Prädikat „regional" bereits zu groß.

Dank der Hilfe zur Selbsthilfe erweist sich die Einwohnerschaft wieder mehr als stabil. Zudem darf sich die Gemeinde inzwischen offiziell zu den „Schönsten Dörfern Italiens" zählen. Und so deutet für Santo Stefano – anders als in besagtem Annaud-Film – alles auf ein Happy End!

<<< Facts: Architektur-Biennale 2012: Hätten Sextantio Restauri Italiani ein Landgut in der Toskana oder ein Quartier in Rom in Stand gesetzt, würde wahrscheinlich kein Hahn danach krähen. Für so etwas ist die behutsame Erneuerung seit Jahrzehnten erprobt. Mit derselben Methode ein ganzes Dorf wiederzubeleben, ist dagegen neu und politisch relevant. Also durften sie ihre Arbeiten auf einer kurz zurückliegenden Architektur-Biennale zeigen. Auf der Weltmesse der Baukunst repräsentierte Santo Stefano ganz Italien.

Booking information:

Via Principe Umberto

I-67020 Santo Stefano di Sessanio

T +39 (0)862 / 89 91 12

F +39 (0)862 / 89 96 56

reservation@sextantio.it

www.sextantio.it

Natur/
nature

★ Superbude St. Pauli

Juliusstraße 1–7 | D-22769 Hamburg

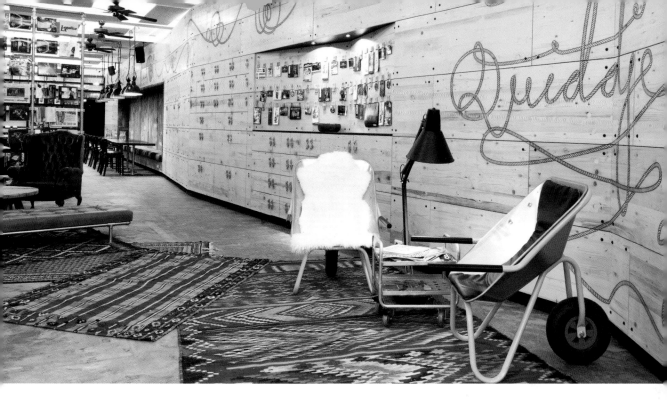

There is a clash between coffee brown and blue-and-white. It is impossible, at the football grounds, to cheer for HSV and support the team from Millerntor at the same time. Even the most extreme of football fans wouldn't dream of it. It is with good reason that the football club banner flaps below a pirate flag. Those who live in St. Pauli are often caught in the stranglehold of the respectable Hanseatic city. A look at the map reveals why: The neighbourhood is sandwiched between the enterprising Hafen-City and the middle-class hinterland around the Elbchaussee. Consequently, St.Pauli has always sought to make the most of its awkward location. It is different and proud of it! It takes small and big liberties with regard to city planning. The squatting in Hafenstraße, as well as the extravagant pleasures of the Reeperbahn, bear witness to this.

These sites are only a few steps away from the accommodation in question. The Superbude St. Pauli, on the threshold of the Schanzenviertel, fits perfectly into this neighbourhood. Also in terms of price: apart from double, four-bed and six-bed rooms, there are backpacker beds that hardly cost more than a day ticket for Hamburg's public transport.

Ist ambience reflects the multicultural mix of the neighbourhood. The interior is clad with yellowing cheap boarding, a reminder of its past as a post office. The interior designers DREIMETA, who designed the first Superbude in Hamburg St. Georg, once again thought up a whole host of quirky details: seating areas are upholstered with old jeans, wheelbarrows serve as chairs, beer crates as bar stools, cable drums as tables. Localist newspapers are used as wallpaper, souvenir anchors hang from toilet plungers as coat hangers. Everything about St. Pauli screams that it is not Hamburg.

<<< Facts: Superbude is dominated by the yellow colour of its panelling. The creators at DREIMETA are of the opinion: "The colour is very funny. People are always laughing. The sun shines all the time here, which, in Hamburg, isn't so often. It's a good mood." Surface 7/2012

Kaffeebraun und Blau-Weiß beißen sich. Im Volkspark den HSV anzufeuern und zugleich mit der FC St. Pauli zu fiebern, ist ein Ding der Unmöglichkeit. Kein noch so Fußball verrückter Fan käme auf diese Idee. Die Anhänger der Mannschaft vom Millerntor segeln nicht umsonst unter der Piratenflagge.

Wer in St. Pauli wohnt, sieht sich nicht selten im Würgegriff der wohlanständigen Hanseaten. Der Blick auf die Karte bestätigt diese Sicht: Der Kiez ist eingeklemmt zwischen der geschäftstüchtigen Hafen-City und dem gutbürgerlichen Hinterland der Elbchaussee. Also macht St. Pauli seit jeher das beste aus seiner prekären Lage: Es ist anders! Längst haben sich die Kleine und die Große Freiheit in den Stadtplan eingeschrieben. Heute künden die Hausbesetzungen der Hafenstraße davon genauso wie die ausschweifenden Vergnügungen der Reeperbahn. Von solchen Schauplätzen bedarf es nur wenige Schritte bis zum Nachtlager. Die Superbude St. Pauli, die auf der Schwelle zum Schanzenviertel liegt, passt da perfekt. Auch preislich: Ihre Backpacker-Betten, die neben Doppel-, Vierer- oder Sechser-Zimmern angeboten werden, kosten kaum mehr als die Tageskarte des Hamburger Verkehrsverbunds. Das Ambiente bringt den Multikulti-Kiez auf den Punkt. Billige Schalbretter kleiden das Haus aus, gelblich imprägniert erinnern sie an seine Vergangenheit als Postamt. Aufs Neue haben sich die Interieur-Designer von DREIMETA, die schon die erste Superbude in St. Georg einrichteten, jede Menge aberwitziger Details ausgedacht: Alte Jeans polstern Sitzecken aus; Schubkarren dienen als Sessel, Bierkästen als Hocker, Kabeltrommeln als Tische; lokalpatriotische Zeitungen wurden zur Tapete; Souvenir-Anker, die als Garderobe fungieren, hängen an Klo-Prömpeln. Alles schreit: St. Pauli ist nicht Hamburg.

<<< Facts: Das Gelb von Schalbrettern beherrscht die Superbude. Die Macher von DREIMETA meinen dazu: „The color is very funny. People are always laughing. The sun shines all the time here, which, in Hamburg, isn't so often. It's a good mood."
Surface 7/2012

Booking information:

Juliusstraße 1–7

D-22769 Hamburg

T +49 (0)40 / 807 91 58 20

stpauli@superbude.de

www.superbude.de/hostel-hamburg-st-pauli

Stadt/
city

★ THE PROPOSAL

Dubsstrasse 33 a | CH-8003 Zurich

Art, life – two words, one thought: there has to be a connection between the two! Up until now such connections have been represented by shops, where artists exhibited their work and their daily lives, or Livecams that broadcast peculiarities on the world wide web. However, the connection between art and life was never complete. There was always something dividing them.

THE PROPOSAL breaks down the last boundaries. The Swiss gallery for art occupies a backstreet in the Zurich district of Wiedikon and provides a "residence in art" during art installations. The creators Jeremie, Lenny and Christian offer bagel breakfasts and a total of two beds. The first is located in a separate room in the gallery itself in the piano nobile of the main building. Breakfast is served on the piano level of the gallery with direct view on the exhibition on display. Around 250 guests so far have dared to spend the night there. For those who are lwho are more adventures, there is an old Peugeot J7 parked in the yard. The bus, made in 1977, was carefully refurbished and stylishly converted. the bus was a former ultraregional art televison chanel, a whole in one tv-studio and broadcasting

unit called WATCHY WALKY TV founded by the owners (www.watchywalky.tv) .Apart from the front, all the sides are painted in matt silver, including the windows. The interior, mostly made of plywood, contains just a double bed. Whether what goes on in there can be regarded as art is revealed by gull-wing doors, or not ...

<<< Facts: "At THE PROPOSAL, art meets hospitality. Since last November, at Dubsstrasse 33 in Zurich, there is a new Mecca for sleepy art enthusiasts or for sleep fanatics interested in art." Kinki Magazine, January 2012

Kunst Leben – zwei Worte, ein Gedanke: eine Verbindung muss es geben! Radikalste Realisierungen waren bisher Ladenlokale, in denen sich Künstler samt ihres Alltags ausstellten, oder Livecams, die mehr oder minder Ungewohntes im World Wide Web verbreiteten. Allein: Die Verbindung zwischen Kunst und Leben war nie total. Mindestens eine Trennscheibe blieb.

Die letzten Schranken nieder reißt THE PROPOSAL. Die Schweizer Kunstgalerie besetzt einen Hinterhof im Züricher Stadtteil Wiedikon und hält sich während der Kunstinstallationen als „residence in art" bereit. Bei den Machern Jeremie, Lenny und Christian findet jedermann ein Bagel-Frühstück sowie insgesamt zwei Betten. Das erste liegt in einem separaten Zimmer der Kunstgalerie im piano nobile des Haupthauses. Frühstück wird in den Ausstellungsräumen gereicht. An die 250 Gäste hatten bereits den Mut, dort zu ruhen. Wer noch abenteuerlustiger ist, für den parkt im Hof ein alter Peugeot J7. Der Bus, Baujahr 1977 und ursprünglich im Einsatz für den Fernsehsender WatchyWalkyTV, wurde sorgsam aufgearbeitet und stilvoll umgestaltet. Bis auf die Front sind sämtliche Seiten mattsilber lackiert, Fenster inklusive. Das weitgehend mit Sperrholz ausgeschlagene Interieur besteht ausschließlich aus einem Doppelbett. Ob als Kunst gelten kann, was sich darauf abspielt, verraten Flügeltüren. Oder auch nicht ...

<<< Facts: „Bei THE PROPOSAL trifft Kunst auf Gastfreundschaft: Seit vergangenem November gibt es also an der Dubsstrasse 33 a in Zürich ein neues Mekka für verschlafene Kunstfans oder kunstinteressierte Schlaffanatiker."
Kinki Magazin, Januar 2012

Booking information:

Dubsstrasse 33 a

CH-8003 Zurich

T +41 (0)43 243 89 84

info@theproposal.cc

www.theproposal.cc

Stadt/
city

★ **Treehotel**

Edeforsvägen 2 a | SE-960 24 Harads

Everything is rocking. The trunk is swaying in the wind and our abode is vibrating. The forest is holding us in suspense. We are being held aloft by an ancient treetop! That is the charm of any treehouse, the charm of nature.

Of course this charm is gaining ever wider appeal as human culture develops further. In the meantime the treehouse has mutated into a mass product, based on rustic retro design. Such holiday residences are proliferating everywhere, especially in Western Europe. The forest has become inundated with treehouses.

Britta and Kent Jonsson-Lindvall offer something quite different: They own a forest with wide open views! The sloped location looks over a river valley that emanates from the depths of the Arctic Circle and flows into the Baltic Sea at Lulea, Sweden's northern-most provincial capital. The local architects were ready to pounce on such a view, and they put forward a whole string of treehouse designs. The only guide-lines were ecological elements that are standard nowadays: They were to be built with wood and run using local resources.

Sandell Sandberg raised a flame red house onto a platform. Mårten and Gustav Cyrén appended the deck of a ship between the tree trunks. Bolle Tham and Martin Videgård suspended a fully mirrored cube from the treetops. The Inredningsgruppen under Bertil Harström weaved branches into a bird's nest and made a UFO hover next to it!

This resulted in a unique collection. Treehotel runs the treehouse as an avant-garde way of life. It remains to be seen whether it will become mainstream. Lovers of nostalgia will feel quite at home here. Britta's Pensionat is the base camp for the treehouse, it is the epitome of cosiness and also highly original. It originated during the heyday of swing.

<<< Facts: The founders Britta and Kent Lindvall are already realising other models of this kind of treehouses.

Alles swingt. Der Stamm wiegt sich im Wind und unser Heim vibriert. Der Wald hält uns in Atem. Wir tragen die älteste Krone der Welt und sie trägt uns! Das ist der Reiz jedes Baumhauses, der Reiz unserer Natur selbst.

Natürlich wächst dieser Reiz, je weiter sich die menschliche Kultur fortentwickelt. Derweil mutiert das Baumhaus zum Massenprodukt, das erst rustikales Retro-Design erdet. Solche Feriendomizile wuchern allenthalben, vor allem in Westeuropa. Fast sieht man den Wald vor lauter Baumhäusern nicht mehr.

Ganz anders bei Britta und Kent Jonsson-Lindvall: Sie besitzen einen Wald mit Weitblick! Die Handlage schaut auf ein Flusstal, das den Tiefen des Polarkreises entspringt und bei Lulea, Schwedens nördlichster Provinzhauptstadt, in die Ostsee mündet. Auf eine solche Aussicht hatten die Architekten der Region nur gelauert. Reihenweise lieferten sie Baumhausentwürfe. Einzige Vorgaben waren ökologische Kunstgriffe, die heute Usus sind: Bauen mit Holz, Betrieb mit den Ressourcen am Ort.

Sandell Sandberg hob ein feuerrotes Haus-vom-Nikolaus aufs Podest. Mårten und Gustav Cyrén spannten ein Schiffsdeck zwischen die Stämme. Bolle Tham und Martin Videgård hängten einen vollver-spiegelten Würfel unter die Kiefernkronen. Die Inredningsgruppen um Bertil Harström flocht Äste zu einem Vogelnest und brachte daneben ein UFO zum Schweben!

So entstand eine einzigartige Kollektion. Das Treehotel führt das Baumhaus als avantgardistische Lebensform vor. Ob das morgen Mainstream ist, wird sich zeigen. Nebenbei kommen auch Nostalgiefreunde auf ihre Kosten. Als Basislager des Treehotels dient das Pensionat. Die erste Adresse der Baumhausherrin ist eine Ausgeburt an Gemütlichkeit und ebenfalls ein echtes Original. Es stammt just aus der Zeit, da der Swing auf seinem Höhepunkt war.

<<< Facts: Schon jetzt realisieren die Gründer Britta und Kent Lindvall weitere Exemplare der Treehotels.

Booking information:

Edeforsvägen 2 a

SE-960 24 Harads

T +46 (0)928 / 104 03

info@treehotel.se, booking@treehotel.se

www.treehotel.se

Natur/
nature

★ Utter Inn

Kopparbergsvägen 1 | SE-722 13 Västerås

Captain Nemo meets Noah! It is in fact you who brings the two together, by playing the role of the two famous characters from classical adventure stories in real life! In any case, the place where this memorable event takes place is very real. The first anchor point is Västerås. The wealthy and polished industrial town lies about an hour's drive west of Stockholm. The two metropolises are linked by Sweden's third largest lake, Mälaren, which covers no less than 1,000 square kilometres. It is right in the middle of this inland sea that the designer Mikael Genberg placed the Utter Inn (otter hotel) in 2000. While otters normally live on land, the hotel is anchored in the water. It is accessed by shuttle boat and initially appears as a bright red dot on the horizon. The ark, with a main deck of 25 square metres, has typically Scandinavian features. If you peer through the port-holes, the interior is unremarkable, until you notice the staircase. Three metres below lies the Utter Inn, as a veritable submarine! Captain Nemo would most certainly have approved: panoramic windows flanking the two beds afford insights into the underwater world. Occasionally a smelt swims past. The gently rolling waves lull you to sleep. There is still space in the logbook, perhaps for new world literature ...

<<< Facts: Mikael Genberg: In contrast to the Utter Inn, the Swedish artist's work is normally aimed skywards. The Café Koala in Rio de Janeiro is made of five-metre-high chairs. The Hotel Woodpecker is located in the highest tree in Västerås. Genberg is currently planning something similar on the moon! There was already a trial run in 2009, on the roof of the world.

Kapitän Nemo trifft Noah! Und Sie sind live dabei, ja Sie bringen die zwei sogar erst zusammen: In Personalunion spielen Sie diese beiden Giganten des klassischen Abenteuerromans – und das im wahren Leben!

Höchst real ist jedenfalls der Ort, an dem dieses denkwürdige Ereignis stattfindet. Den ersten Ankerpunkt bildet Västerås. Die ebenso wohlhabende wie aufgeräumte Industriestadt liegt gut eine Autostunde westlich von Stockholm. Beide Metropolen verbindet Schwedens drittgrößter See: der Mälaren, dessen weit ausufernde Küsten nicht weniger als 1.000 Quadratkilometer umschließen. Mitten in eben dieses Binnenmeer setzte der Design-künstler Mikael Genberg im Jahr 2000 das Utter Inn (das Otter-Hotel).

Während Otter gewöhnlich an Land hausen, ist das Hotel auf dem Wasser verankert. Die Anreise erfolgt im Shuttleboot und offenbart zuerst einen knallroten Punkt am Horizont. Zwischen Garage und Hundehütte bewegt sich, was auf dem von 25 Quadratmeter großen Basisdeck steht: Die Arche zeigt typisch skandinavische Züge. Wer durch die Bullaugen blickt, sieht nur das Nötigste – bis sich diese Treppe auftut! Drei Meter tiefer entpuppt sich das Utter Inn als veri-tables U-Boot! Was Kapitän Nemo sicher zugesagt hätte: Längs und quer der beiden Betten gestatten Panoramafenster Einblicke in die Unterwasserwelt. Ab und an schwimmt ein Stint vorbei. Derweil treibt der stete sanfte Wellengang zum Träumen. Das Logbuch bietet noch Platz, für neue Weltliteratur zum Beispiel ...

<<< Facts: Mikael Genberg: Anders als beim Utter Inn strebt der schwedische Künstler mit seinem Œuvre gewöhnlich gen Himmel. So besteht das Café Koala in Rio de Janeiro aus fünf Meter hohen Stühlen. Das Hotel Woodpecker findet seinen Platz im höchsten Baum von Västerås. Ähnliches plant Genberg gegenwärtig auf dem Mond! Einen Testlauf gab es schon: 2009, auf dem Dach der Welt.

Booking information:

Kopparbergsvägen 1

SE-722 13 Västerås

T +46 (0)21 / 39 01 00

malarstaden@vasteras.se

www.visitvasteras.se/

aktor/hotell-utter-inn

Stadt/
city

Natur/
nature

★ **V8 Hotel**

Graf-Zeppelin-Platz | D-71034 Böblingen

A boy is lining up his toy cars. When he's grown up, he'll buy one make after another, for real! This is how the website mobile.de advertises itself. It would be very costly to fulfil one's childhood dreams by means of the second-hand car market. Especially compared to the cost of staying at the V8 Hotel, where the originals even serve as beds for car enthusiasts!

The V8 Hotel is located in Stuttgart, where Mercedes and Porsche are manufactured and have monumental museums. The hotel is directly adjacent to the Meilenwerk, which showcases the history of all makes of automobile. The main building is that of the former Böblingen airport, built in 1928 in the Bauhaus style, which already comprised a hotel at that time. Photographic posters act as reminders of its aeronautical past, especially in the Zeppelin Suite occupying half of the tower.

The hotel displays its fetish with cars very strikingly. There are oldtimers all over the hotel. In a number of rooms there is the faint waft of petrol. The car theme is especially dominant in the ten themed rooms. In the "Workshop" the sleeping area is raised up on a hydraulic ramp and a workbench serves as the dressing table. In the "Carwash", one's head rests on the giant brushes and its hot air current replaces a hairdryer. The "Motor Racing" apartment features a winners' podium and Formula One tyres. The "Petrol Station" has a petrol pump instead of a minibar. The "Drive-in Cinema" features a pay kiosk wardrobe, an artificial starry sky and a cadillac that has been converted into a bed. Its ignition is no longer needed …

<<< Facts: "My husband planned this trip as it was his weekend for car spotting. I just came along for the ride. As a result I really had no idea where we were staying, until the sat nav directed us into what looked like a car museum. This place is amazing." Victoria Switzerland, TripAdvisor

Ein Junge schreitet seine Spielzeug-Autos ab. Groß geworden, wird er ein Modell nach dem anderen erwerben, in echt! Mit diesem Spot preist sich mobile.de an. Den Jugendtraum via Gebrauchtwagenmarkt zu erfüllen, ist freilich ein teures Vergnügen. Vor allem im Vergleich zum V8 Hotel. Und hier begleiten die Originale den Autofreund sogar bis unter die Bettdecke!

Das V8 Hotel findet sich, wo sich Mercedes und Porsche mit monumentalen Museen produzieren: in Stuttgart. Sein Standort liegt unmittelbar neben dem Meilenwerk, das markenunabhängig die Automobilgeschichte wieder aufleben lässt. Sein Haupthaus ist das des ehemaligen Flughafens Böblingen, das 1928 im Bauhaus-Stil entstand und schon damals ein Hotel barg. An die aeronautische Vergangenheit erinnern Fotoplakate – vorrangig in der Zeppelin-Suite, welche den halben Turm einnimmt.

Noch markanter wird der Fetisch Fahrzeug in Szene gesetzt. Oldtimer sind in dem Hotel allgegenwärtig. Sämtliche Räume durchzieht ein dezenter Benzingeruch. Besonders präsent ist er in den zehn Themenzimmern: In der „Werkstatt" ist das Nachtlager auf einer Hebebühne aufgebockt, der Sekretär besteht aus einer Werkbank. Bei „Carwash" wird der Kopf auf die riesigen Bürsten einer Waschstraße gebettet, deren Gebläse den Fön ersetzt. Das „Rennsport"Apartment kombiniert Siegertreppchen und Formel-1-Reifen. In der „Tankstelle" gibt es eine Zapfsäule anstelle der Minibar. Das „Autokino" bietet einen Kassenhäuschen-Kleiderschrank, einen künstlichen Sternenhimmel und einen Cadillac, der von vorne herein zum Bett umfunktioniert ist. Einen Zündschlüssel braucht es da nicht mehr ...

<<< Facts: Das V8 Hotel ist mit viel Liebe zum Detail gestaltet. In den Themenzimmern fehlt selbst der dezente Geruch von Motoröl statt Benzingeruch nicht.

Booking information:

Graf-Zeppelin-Platz

D-71034 Böblingen

T +49 (0)7031 / 306 98 80

F +49 (0)7031 / 306 98 88 88

info@v8hotel.de

www.v8hotel.de

Stadt/   Natur/
city   nature

★ Verladeturm

Hafenstraße 1 a | D-15324 Groß Neuendorf

People in freight wagons!?! Especially in Germany, this may well set the alarm bells ringing. In Groß Neuendorf its historical connotations have been replaced by a more conciliatory meaning. The community of 500 souls lies in the Oderbruch area, amidst almost 1,000 square kilometres of marshland, which only became habitable in the mid-eighteenth century when the river was regulated.

In the meantime, the Oderbruch railway and port increased the number of inhabitants five-fold and made the outpost a strategic transhipment point. However, not long after the German expansionism in the Second World War had been defeated, all that remained of this was a stagnant area in the border territory between Germany and Poland. It was only after the two countries were united under the banner of the European Union that things were set to change. The joint redevelopment company DePoRe initiated the refurbishment of the port for tourism. The most striking section was restored by the Berlin architect Jens Plate: the loading tower from 1940 was converted into a museum café. A four-storey holiday maisonette with a skylight was created under its roof. Eight-metre-long swings were suspended from the conveyor bridge. These and the viewing platform afford contemplative views over the meandering Oder river. The freight wagons, into which Jens Plate installed three modest accommodation units, are an even more unusual experience. Without leaving the accommodation, you can fish in the Oder. Owing to the exposed east-facing location, the very first rays of morning sunshine fall on the double bed and light up the changes brought by the new era.

<<< Facts: The joint redevelopment company DePoRe initiated the refurbishment of the port for tourism. The most striking section was restored by Jens Plate Architekten in 2005.

Booking information:

Hafenstraße 1 a

D-15324 Groß Neuendorf

T +49 (0)30 / 50 56 24 71

F +49 (0)30 / 50 56 24 72

info@verladeturm.de

www.verladeturm.de

Natur/
nature

Menschen in Güterwaggons!?! Gerade in Deutschland mögen da die Alarmglocken angehen – in Groß Neuendorf nicht. Die 500-Seelen-Gemeinde liegt im Oderbruch, inmitten von fast 1.000 Quadratkilometern Sumpf, welcher durch die Regulierung des Flusses in der Mitte des 18. Jahrhunderts überhaupt erst bewohnbar wurde.

Zwischenzeitlich mochten Oderbruchbahn und Hafen die Einwohnerzahl verfünffachen und den Außenposten zum strategischen Umschlagplatz adeln. Doch davon blieb, kaum dass die germanische Expansionspolitik im Zweiten Weltkrieg vernichtend geschlagen worden war, nur mehr ein Stillleben im Grenzland zwischen Deutschland und Polen. Erst nachdem beide Länder unter dem Dach der Europäischen Union zusammenfanden, kam Änderung in Sicht.

Die gemeinsame Entwicklungsgesellschaft DePoRe initiierte die Erneuerung des Hafens für den Fremdenverkehr. Den markantesten Teil erwarb und restaurierte der Berliner Architekt Jens Plate: Der Verladeturm von 1940 wandelte sich zum Museumscafé.

Unter seinem Dach entstand eine vierstöckige Ferienmaisonette mit Skylight. An die Förderbrücke wurden acht Meter lange Schaukeln gehängt. Spielgerät und Aussichtsplattform selbst bieten einen kontemplativen Blick über alle Windungen des Oderbruchs.

Noch intensiver ist der Genuss in den Güterwaggons, in denen Plate drei bescheidene Unterkünfte einrichtete. Ohne das Nachtlager zu verlassen, lässt sich in der Oder angeln. Dank der exponierten Ostlage berühren schon die ersten Sonnenstrahlen das Doppelbett. In ganz Deutschland merkt kaum jemand früher, was die neue Zeit geschlagen hat.

<<< Facts: 2005 erfolgte die Sanierung des alten Verladeturms im Hafen Groß Neuendorf durch Jens Plate Architekten.

★ Vuurtoren

Havenweg 1 | NL-8861 XH Harlingen

The storm is lashing the waves over the tidal flats, lightning is striking every second. The sea is very turbulent tonight. It is only the lighthouse that is a bastion of calm. Nobody need be concerned about Harlingen …

Even its style suggests safety: The art deco top adds a playful touch to the cubist shaft. Until the architect Jelsma took charge of the 25-metre-high structure in 1920, real beacon fires burned at the top. Piloting ships to Harlingen was a challenging and important task. The trade that they brought made the Hanseatic city rich.

However, the lighthouse was powerless against the silting up of the port, which had to be circumnavigated via a new water channel, making the Harlingen beacons superfluous just before the turn of the millennium. However, the tower stayed in use as accommodation for two, with sweeping views.

The present-day lighthouse attendant leads you through a hallway that would befit a traditional administrative building, but which in fact exhibits the lighting engineering of the past. On the penultimate level, guests can refresh themselves in the bathroom. The thoughtfully converted living room area is located above it. The glazing all around, under the copper dome of the lighthouse, has remained. A ladder with a safety cage leads up to the highest viewpoint. Over the balustrades there are views towards sunny Harlingen: the picture-postcard Netherlands!

<<< Facts: "In February 1998 the fire was extinguished. For centuries, seafarers had looked towards the lighthouse. Now the roles have been nicely reversed: The beacon has become a viewpoint." Piet Beuker, Harlinger, lighthouse keeper (1970–1998)

Booking information:

Havenweg 1

NL-8861 XH Harlingen

T +31 (0)517 / 414410

info@dromenaanzee.nl

www.vuurtoren-harlingen.nl

Meer/   Natur/
ocean   nature

Der Sturm peitscht die Wellen über das Watt, Blitze zucken im Sekundentakt. Die See ist heute Nacht höchst aufgewühlt. Wie ein Fels in der Brandung steht allein der Leuchtturm. Um Harlingen muss sich niemand sorgen ...
Sicherheit suggeriert schon der Stil: Die Art-Deco-Spitze gibt dem kubistischen Schaft eine verspielte Note. Bis Kommunalarchitekt Jelsma den gut 25 Meter hohen Bau 1920 in Angriff nahm, brannten an selber Stelle echte Leuchtfeuer. Damit Schiffe nach Harlingen zu lotsen, war ein hochsensibler Akt. Der Handel, den sie brachten, machte die Hansestadt reich.
Gegen eines war allerdings auch der Turm machtlos: die Verlandung des Hafens. Sie war nur durch eine neue Fahrrinne zu umgehen, die kurz vor dem Millennium das Harlinger Leuchtfeuer überflüssig machte. Der Turm blieb dennoch in Betrieb: als aussichtsreiches Nachtlager für zwei. Die heutige Leuchtturmwärterin führt durch ein Treppenhaus, das eines ausgewachsenen Verwaltungsbaus würdig wäre, tatsächlich aber die Lichttechnik von einst ausstellt. In der Etage unter der Spitze können sich die Gäste frisch machen: Hier ist das Bad untergebracht. Darüber befindet sich der detailverliebt umgestaltete Wohnbereich. Geblieben ist die Rundum-Verglasung, welche sich im Leuchtfeuerhaus unter der Kupferkuppel findet.
Auf die höchste Aussicht führt allein eine Steigleiter. Wenn es eintrifft, hat sich der Wind für gewöhnlich längst gelegt. Die Balustrade gibt den Blick frei auf das sonnige Harlingen: Holland wie aus dem Bilderbuch!

<<< Facts: „**Im Februar 1998 löschte ich das Feuer. Jahrhundertelang haben die Seeleute in diese Richtung geschaut. Jetzt sind die Rollen schön umgedreht: Die Bake ist zum Aussichtspunkt geworden."**
Piet Beuker, Harlinger Leuchtturmwärter von 1970–1998

★ **Whitepod**

Route des Cerniers, CP 681 | CH-1871 Les Giettes

What can be more divine than falling snow ... This is what a lot of people think, looking out of the window, while sitting indoors in the warmth. The snowflakes slowly pirouette down towards the earth.

The Whitepod offers just such an experience. It is located in the western Alps, near the Swiss-French border, at 1,700 metres above sea level. There is an abundance of snow, which can be enjoyed on seven kilometres of pistes of varying difficulty levels, with two private ski lifts. It envelopes the visitor almost completely during the winter season. The shelters look like snowballs. There are 15 geodetic domes, each 40 square metres in size, within which up to four people can snuggle up to each other. A permanently glowing fireplace, two well-insulated tent layers and an array of fleecy fabrics ensure warmth for the guests.

However, the real highlight are the platforms that support the Whitepods on the slope and keep the views free of snow. From the double bed one can see 1,300 metres down to the deep blue of Lake Geneva, with Montreux's thousand sparkling lights on its shore.

<<< Facts: Lake Geneva:

It is definitely worth visiting Lake Geneva, which can be seen from the Whitepod. From the beginning of March to the end of July, three international music festivals take place around the lake: the "Montreux Choral Festival", the "Nuits du Jazz de Cherne" and, last but not least, the "Montreux Jazz Festival".

Es geht doch nichts über fallenden Schnee ... So mag der Betrachter denken, der wohl gewärmt hinter der Fensterscheibe sitzt. Was für ein fataler Irrtum, das wahre Schauspiel erlebt die Schneeflocke selbst! In überirdischen Höhen kuscheln sich ihre Kristalle aneinander. Kälte ist da kein Thema. Und der freie Fall federt sich soweit ab, bis die Erde auf die Schneeflocke zuzutanzen scheint!

Ebendieses Erlebnis bietet das Whitepod. Es befindet sich in den Westalpen, nahe der Grenze, an der aus der Schweiz Frankreich wird, und liegt 1.700 Meter über Normal-Null. Schnee, der mit zwei Privatliften und Sieben-Kilometer-Pisten verschiedener Schwierigkeitsgrade hautnah ausgekostet werden kann, gibt es hier reichlich. Fast vollkommen schließt er den Besucher während der Wintersaison ein.

Wie Schneekugeln sehen auch die Behausungen aus. Tatsächlich handelt es sich um 15 geodätische Kuppeln, unter deren je 40 Quadratmetern sich bis zu vier Personen aneinander kuscheln können. Ein permanent prasselnder Kamin, zwei wohl isolierte Zeltlagen und allerlei flauschige Raumtextilien sorgen zusätzlich dafür, dass den Bewohnern stets warm ist.

Der eigentliche Clou aber sind die Plattformen, welche die Whitepods über dem Hang und ihre Aussicht schneefrei halten. Vom Doppelbett aus stürzt der Blick 1,300 Meter hinab, auf das tiefe Blau des Genfer Sees, von dessen Ufer Montreux mit seinen Abertausend Lichtern aufblitzt. Jede Wette: Da werden sogar die Schneeflocken neidisch!

<<< Facts: Genfer See:
Was das Whitepod im Blick hat, ist garantiert einen Besuch wert – gerade wenn der Schnee schmilzt. Von Anfang März bis Ende Juli finden rund um den Genfer See drei Musik-Festivals von internationalem Rang statt: das „Montreux Choral Festival", die „Nuits du Jazz de Cherne" und last, not least das „Montreux Jazz Festival".

Booking information:

Route des Cerniers, CP 681

CH-1871 Les Giettes

T +41 (0)24 / 471 38 38

F +41 (0)24 / 471 39 55

info@whitepod.com

www.whitepod.com

Berge/
hills

Natur/
nature

★ **Yotel Heathrow**

Arrivals Mezzanine Landside, Terminal 4, London Heathrow Airport | UK-TW6 3XA Hounslow, Middlesex

In Steven Spielberg's 2004 film "Terminal", Tom Hanks is stranded at the airport for months. He sleeps, eats and works in the transit area and even arranges rendezvous.

Real life has progressed a little further in the meantime. Three years after the film, the Yotel Heathrow was opened in Terminal 4. The modern converted space within the arrivals hall now provides all that is required to ensure that time spent in transit is pleasant. Soundproofed cubicles comprise at least one bed, a bathroom for refreshing showers, a workspace with state-of-the-art communications technology and smart storage space, while only measuring seven square metres on average. Catering is a luxury form of typical airline fare. Booking, check-in and check-out are all electronic. It is payable by the hour or by the day, so you can arrive and leave spontaneously. The majority of customers don't come out of necessity, but out of choice.

Just one location is not enough to meet the requirements of mobile guests and so similar establishments are popping up in airports everywhere, from Amsterdam to Munich, Moscow and New Delhi. The Superbox, opened recently in New York, stands virtually in the middle of Times Square!

<<< Facts: Lost in Transition: If capsule hotels have a homeland, then it is Japan. The prototype stands in Osaka and has been in operation since 1979. Its design by Kisho Kurokawa is a masterpiece of Japanese Metabolism. Its countless epigones are merely stacks of boxes of barely two and a half cubic metres, often used in Japan's red light districts. The opened imitations in Xi'an in China, or in Singapore, hardly afford any privacy.

<<< Facts: Lost in Transition: Wenn Kapsel-hotels eine Heimat haben, so ist es Japan. Der Prototyp steht in Osaka, wo er seit 1979 in Betrieb ist. Mit ihm entwarf Kisho Kurokawa ein Meisterwerk des Metabolismus. Seine zahllosen Epigonen beschränkten sich auf Stapel von kaum zweieinhalb Kubikmeter großen Boxen, die nicht selten in Nippons Rotlichtvierteln Verwendung finden. Kaum Privatsphäre bieten auch jene Ableger, die in Xi'an, China, oder in Singapur eröffneten.

Noch reichlich holprig strandet Tom Hanks 2004 in Steven Spielbergs' „Terminal". Monatelang kommt er nicht aus dem Flughafen raus: Er schläft, isst, arbeitet in der Transitzone und arrangiert sogar Rendezvous – ohne dass sie sich auch nur ansatzweise darauf einrichten will.

Die Wirklichkeit ist mittlerweile weiter: Drei Jahre nach dem Film öffnete im Terminal 4 das Yotel Heathrow. Der modern umgestaltete Restraum der Ankunftshalle offeriert nun alles, was für eine angenehme Zwischenzeit nötig ist. Schalldichte Kapseln bieten mindestens einen Schlafplatz, ein Bad für stürmisches Duschen, einen Arbeitsplatz mit zeitgemäßer Kommunikationstechnik sowie pfiffigen Stauraum. Dabei messen sie im Standardmaß gerade sieben Quadratmeter.

Als Verpflegung gibt es die Luxusvariante typischen Flugzeugessens. Buchung, Check-In und Check-Out erfolgen elektronisch. Abgerechnet wird tage- oder stundenweise. So kann der Aufenthalt extrem spontan begonnen und beendet werden. Tatsächlich kommt die Mehrheit der Besucher nicht mehr notgedrungen, sondern aus freien Stücken.

Zur Optimierung auf den mobilen Gast gehört auch, dass eine einzelne Destination nicht genügen kann. Und so wächst Vergleichbares allenthalben aus den Rollfeldern: von Amsterdam über München und Moskau bis Neu Delhi. Yotel selbst geht derweil einen anderen Weg und holt die Gäste da ab, wo sie sein wollen. Die Superbox, die jüngst in New York eröffnete, steht quasi mitten auf dem Times Square!

Booking information:

Arrivals Mezzanine Landside

Terminal 4

London Heathrow Airport

UK-TW6 3XA Hounslow,

Middlesex

T +44 (0)207 / 100 11 00

customer@yotel.com

Stadt/
city

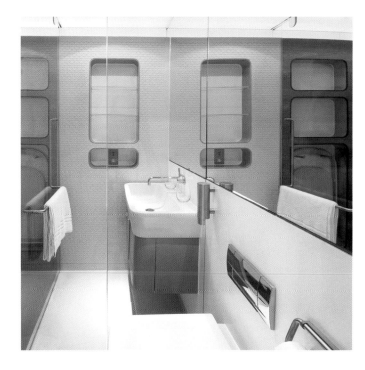

★ Notes | Notizen

PHOTO CREDITS | BILDNACHWEIS

Cover | Titelseite:
Treehotel: Peter Lundstrom

Introduction | Vorwort:
Treehotel: Peter Lundstrom

andel's Hotel Lodz: Harald Eisenberger
Apafi Manor: MET – The Mihai Eminescu Trust, Ionit Macri
ArkaBarka Floating Hostel: Ivan Topalovic
Arte Luise Kunsthotel: Arte Luise Kunsthotel
Atomium – Kids Sphere: www.atomium.be, SABAM 2009
Attrap'Rêves: Attrap'Rêves
Clavell Tower: The Landmark Trust
Crownhill Fort: The Landmark Trust
CUBE Savognin: Kai Dudenhöfer, Peter Garmusch, Eduard Huebner
Eastern Comfort Hostelboat: Eastern Comfort Hostelboat
Ecopod Boutique Retreat: Jim Milligan
Gothic Temple: The Landmark Trust
Grotte della Città: Mario di Paolo
Havenkraan van Harlingen: Andre Minkema
Hotel Brosundet: Hotel Brosundet
Hüttenpalast Indoor Camping: Jan Brockhaus
Kakslauttanen Arctic Resort: Kakslauttanen Arctic Resort
Kapari Natural Resort: Ventouris Giorgos
Kelebek Hotel: Kelebek Hotel
Kolarbyn Eco-Lodge: Claudia Deglau, Lasse Fredriksson, Skogens Konung, Mikaela Larm
Kruisherenhotel: Etienne van Sloun
Martello Tower: The Landmark Trust
Pixel Tower: Sigrid Rauchdobler, Dietmar Tollerian
Propeller Island City Lodge: Lars Stroschen
Railholiday: Railholiday, Ross Haxton
Reddingsboot: Andre Minkema
Roulotte Retreat: Helen Abraham, Eilidh Berry Fraser
Sala Silvergruva: Jan-Olof Åkerlund, Pappilabild, Jan Storm
Saljoet: Robert Posthumus, Gert Veldhuis
Salt & Sill: Salt & Sill
Santo Stefano: Mario di Paolo
Superbude St. Pauli: Superbude St. Pauli
THE PROPOSAL: Benjamin Hofer
Treehotel: Peter Lundstrom
Utter Inn: Shirley Clifford, Mikael Genberg, Linda Heplinger
V8 Hotel: Frank Hoppe
Verladeturm: Jens Plate Architekten, Monika Fielitz
Vuurtoren: Andre Minkema
Whitepod: Micha Riechsteiner, Whitepod
Yotel Heathrow: Yotel

IMPRINT | IMPRESSUM :

Verlag:
archimappublishers
Kaiser Peters Wormuth GbR
Weimarer Straße 32
DE-10625 Berlin

Text ITexte: Hans Wolfgang Hoffmann
Layout and Graphic Design I Layout und Gestaltung: **archimap**publishers
Translation I Übersetzung: Lynne Kolar-Thompson

Bibliografische Information der Deutschen Bibliothek – Die Deutsche Bibliothek
verzeichnet diese Publikation in der *Deutschen Nationalbibliografie*; detaillierte
bibliografische Daten sind im Internet über http://dhb.ddb.de abrufbar.

ISBN 978-3-940874-67-2
© Copyright 2014
Text und Bild bei Autor und Verlag.
Alle Rechte vorbehalten.
All rights reserved. No part may be reproduced
without permission of the publisher.

 **archimap**publishers